Feel Me Fall

James Morris

Cover design by StoryWonk
Formatting by Polgarus Studio

Copyright @ 2017 James Morris
All Rights Reserved

This is a work of fiction. Names, characters, organizations, places, events, and incidents are either products of the author's imagination or are used fictitiously. Any resemblance to actual persons, living or dead, or actual events is purely coincidental.

No part of this work may be reproduced, or stored in a retrieval system, or transmitted in any form or by any means, electronic, mechanical, photocopying, recording, or otherwise, without written permission of the author.

For Momma-Jan

CHAPTER ONE

I have tried so hard to forget, but memory is a stubborn thing. Memories linger no matter what I do. They're there all the time—and worse. Even my dreams aren't safe. I have vicious nightmares, and they're real—too real—and suddenly I'm *back there*. I can't will them away, I can't squeeze them away, and the more I try, the more they burrow in my head. I want to cut open my skull and dig my fingers into my brain and just pull them out.

I press the Call Nurse button.

This place, this room; it's no better than a white coffin. Sometimes I feel like the walls are closing in on me and I have to remind myself nothing's moving. Nothing at all.

Breathe, I tell myself. Just breathe.

A nurse enters. She's got skin the color of rich walnut. She says, "It's late, you should be asleep."

"I can't." She tilts her head, knowing it's a lie. The truth is I don't want to. "Can I have some coffee?"

"You've got to sleep sometime, honey." She walks over and gently grasps my bandaged hand. "Do you want me to stay with you a while?"

Usually my mom is with me, but she must've had to run home. Reduced to a little girl, I nod.

I close my eyes, but my mind runs and runs. Tubes and fluids enter my body, but there's nothing to stop the anxiety. My heart pounds and sometimes I fear I'm on the cusp of crossing into whatever lies on the other side of sane. Being in the hospital makes it harder. The white walls and sick people only remind me that I am so far from normal. My mom's apartment in Los Angeles is less than five miles away, but it might as well be a million.

The nurse, staff, doctors, everyone; they all know me for one thing. The thing that will define me for the rest of my life. I am a survivor. The only survivor of Air Brazil, the plane that crashed in the Amazon jungle carrying 134 passengers; 37 of them students, teachers, and chaperones from Riverdale Academy High. I used to hear about plane crashes and wondered how the victims felt in the seconds before impact, wondered what it was like to know you were about to die.

Now I know. And I'd give anything not to.

I knew those people from school. Every. Single. One.

They aren't faceless names. They are people and they are dead.

The counselor didn't help, either. She told me not to feel guilty. Survivor's guilt, she called it. She warned I could expect to be angry and sad. I could expect to be confused. I wanted to tell her I was angry and sad and confused long before I got onto that plane.

My counselor told me to write my story down. By writing I could make sense of all that happened. I keep thinking if I remember everything the way I need to that the memories will fade away. That I can accept what happened. I can accept that I survived and everyone else died.

The laptop on my nightstand is waiting for me. I'm scared to touch it.

I was dead to the world and when I came to I was drowning. Water gushed into my mouth and I was tumbling, flailing, not knowing what end was up or down. I heard the sounds of screaming and the roaring of water and then nothingness. Coming up for air, I held something, something rectangular. The seat cushion I was holding kept me afloat. I was in a river and I didn't know why. I kicked and kicked and it made no difference. I never believed in God, an all-powerful being that allowed so many horrible things to happen, but as I saw the rocks up ahead, I prayed.

The current sped faster, churning like boiling water and I thought I was going to die.

I was 17 and I was going to die.

All the time wasted. All the things I never got to do.

I had one thought over and over: *I don't want to die. Someone else, but not me.*

I held onto that seat cushion for dear life and plunged into the rapids. I was a human rag doll. The torrent sucked me into a watery hell and I couldn't breathe; my eyes shut, mouth shut, face tight against the murk, willing everything to stop. I couldn't breathe. I started to panic.

Someone else, but not me.

I needed air, my body screamed for it and I opened my mouth about to take in water when I bubbled up to the surface and gasped. As quickly as I was brought above, I was taken under again. I slammed against the rocks and buried my face deeper into the cushion. I saw nothing, heard nothing, and imagined I was in a womb. I could only wait for the terror to pass. There was no outlet; my fear was so deep and tangible I couldn't scream. It felt like an actual substance that enveloped my body, my brain, my very being. I receded further and further within myself, a dark hole, my entire body a taut muscle.

Suddenly, I took a shot to the head and saw stars. A high-pitched squeal rang in my ears. I fought the growing sensation of darkness that threatened to overcome me, but I knew to give in meant death. I was tempted. So, so tempted. I forced my eyes open and saw the water, the dark water and wondered in that emptiness if I hadn't died already.

My prayer must've been heard.

The water calmed and I was spit out near a bend. I realized I had to give up the cushion, my lifeline—it was holding me back. I let go, cursing myself as it floated away and I swam, giving everything I had. My body had nothing left but I commanded it, willed it, to swim. As I approached the shore, my shoes finally touched bottom and I heaved myself onto land.

I don't know how long I lay there catching my breath. But there is no greater feeling of security than the sensation of the earth beneath your stomach, hands grabbing dirt. The scent of decay and wet leaves smelled like a bouquet. All this time I'd taken the ground beneath me for granted. Now I was thankful for this place to rest.

I was soaked. My jeans pressed against me, my hair drenched, my socks squished against my feet. I didn't understand. I had left on a flight from Los Angeles with a layover in Panama City and then on to Asuncion, Paraguay for a year-end class trip. We were traveling as an inter-disciplinary trip for history, international relations, foreign language and biology. We were going to have the trip of a lifetime.

Then it hit me, a delayed reaction: I almost drowned. I almost died. My body seized and I was overwhelmed. I cried; I didn't even know why or for what, but I sobbed on that little stretch of dirt. I heaved, gasping for breath. Every inhale was a wheeze, and I caught myself hitting the ground, my hands balled into tight fists, pounding and pounding.

Moments passed and I cried myself empty. I told myself: get up. You have to get up.

I placed my hands in the dirt to help me stand and looked around thinking: *What is this place?* There was green everywhere, too much green, and a river the width of three football fields in front of me. The air was heavy, a physical pressure against my skin. I was in the jungle, a tangled web of trees and totally foreign. Any other time, I might've been amazed by its majesty, only now I felt small. Trees towered behind me, the river flowed in front, and I was trapped.

It was then I felt the weight of my cross-body bag. I'd been wearing it the whole time. Not very heavy, I managed to unhook it and was about to open the zipper when I heard screams.

Floating down the river were more people. I wasn't alone! A ripple of joy overtook me until I saw their faces reflecting what I sensed my own might look like—bruised, bleeding, and utterly thrashed.

Exhausted, I shouted my voice hoarse, "Over here!" I waved my hands over my head. "You can do it," I encouraged. "Almost there!"

Some didn't move at all. They floated, faces down, rolling through the current, lost in the rapids, disappearing for far too long. Those were the ones who didn't thrash. Others were swept in the rapids, their screams barely heard over the rushing water only to be silenced on the other end. I was watching people *die*. The bodies were like a slow leak, trickling down the river a few at a time, and yet almost none of them emerged alive on the other side of the rocks. I couldn't save them. They were too far away.

Someone else, but not me.

I didn't mean like this.

Then I saw Viv and my heart nearly stopped.

She struggled in the water, past the rapids, a bobber about to go under. She was never athletic even though she was stick thin. Water gurgled from her mouth and she barely moved. I couldn't bear to lose her. I wouldn't allow it. I was terrified of my own exhaustion, but I jumped into the water and found a strength I never knew. I swam out to her. Her head dipped under the water and I would not let that be the last time I saw my best friend alive. I grasped her flotation cushion and then headed back to shore.

She looked at me, dazed. "Emily, it's you."

"Yes, it's me." I could barely contain my relief.

The sun shone over my head, reflecting in the ripples. "You look like an angel."

I knew Vivian was out of it. "Stop talking now. Just swim. We're going to be okay."

I reached the shore for a second time and pulled her up with me. Once on land, she pulled me into a hug and nothing had ever felt better. Always shorter than me, her face burrowed into my chest and I felt I was protecting an abandoned baby bird. Her inky dark hair, usually so pretty was now plastered to her head, her make-up had washed away, and she was just this tiny thing. Her whole body shivered. "Tell me it's a dream, tell me it's a dream…."

"I wish it was, Viv." I would've stayed hugging her if not for the other people in need of help.

Nico, Viv's immature boyfriend, splashed ashore, his glasses gone, his nose bloody, red streaks smeared across his face. He was panting and heaved over, and I thought he might throw up. We had a history, but there was no time for irritation. Any familiar face was cause for celebration. He seemed surprised to see me. "You made it."

He then eased Viv from my arms and into his.

Further down the river there was movement. It was Derek, all limbs and urgency, his face pockmarked with acne and not a hint of stubble. He splashed onto shore, his fingers digging into sand and he kissed the earth.

Twenty yards away, Ryan Wray followed. One of his prosthetic legs was missing—he'd lost his legs below the knee after contracting a rare case of meningitis a few years earlier—and he crab-walked onto land, his one pant leg empty, wet, and flat. He wasn't alone. He helped guide Mean Molly with him. She was far from mean then, almost drowned, flustered and frantic. Once she got out of the water, she toppled in the mud, curling into a fetal position.

I stayed where I was as Ryan, Molly and Derek staggered along the shore, finally meeting up with us.

There was no time to rest or reflect. The river scattered more survivors along the shore. I pulled in a man and stopped in alarm when I saw that one of his arms had snapped off. I gently laid him down and he didn't even notice until he turned his head. He said with an eerie calm, "That looks painful." I recognized him from the plane. He'd sat a few aisles in front of me and slammed back drinks whenever we hit a patch of turbulence. On land, he didn't even scream. His face was pale and blood spurted in rhythmic pulses from below his shoulder.

"What do we do?" Nico said.

I had no clue. I only knew we needed to do *something*. "Derek, your belt!"

Derek looked from his perch on the mud and shook his head. I couldn't believe it.

"Derek, give me your belt! He's losing too much blood."

Derek, in shock or otherwise, didn't move.

I searched for anything that would act as a tourniquet, but my efforts were in vain. The man's blood had dwindled to a dribble, leaving a red puddle in the mud.

Another woman emerged from the water like a swamp creature, stumbling. We sat her down and she gazed at the water. She had a head injury like mine. Blood ran from her scalp and there was a small spot where her hair had been chafed away. It wasn't a wound. It was a *hole*. Looking closer, I could see something I didn't want to—her skull and what lay within. Her eyelids fluttered and she swayed, falling unconscious. I tried to grab her, but gravity took her to the ground. I nudged her once, twice; she didn't respond. "Wake up," I pleaded. "Please wake up." She never moved again.

I wanted to scream. I wanted to run from this place.

It seemed like a Halloween parade. They had to be in costume or using special effects; the injuries and deaths couldn't be *real*.

They were all too real.

One man drifted to shore, his face down in the water, his wispy gray hair splayed out on the water's surface. We grabbed ahold of him and he was heavy, far too heavy for his slender body. We saw why. The flotation device had kept him afloat, but he'd drowned somewhere along the way.

The last man we helped suffered so many burns his face was charred and etched in pain—I had the horrible thought of grill marks on steak. Once on land he jumped back into the water. Maybe the water had soothed him. I tried to reach out and grab him. "Let me help you!" But he was hysterical, too fast, and we watched as he floated away. I tell myself that he would've probably died anyway.

It's terrible that I only knew them as The Woman, The Old Man, The Man Without an Arm and The Burned Man. Somewhere people knew their names, their histories, secrets and loves. Many of them rested at our feet, their chests still, mouths open. We were among the dead, and I found that we all, consciously or not, distanced ourselves from the horror.

The six of us stood on the shore, a hodgepodge of strained relationships, but I hoped the past meant nothing now. Silence fell over us. My voice felt robotic. "What happened?"

They looked at me as if I was stupid and in that moment I knew.

You've been in a plane crash.

You've been in a plane crash and you survived.

Viv broke down crying. "Where's everyone else?" I asked.

"Where do you think?" said Ryan.

There had been a whole planeload of people, 37 of them from our school including my English teacher, Mr. DeKoning. We couldn't be the only ones left. Things like this didn't happen. At least not to us. To me.

I struggled, trying to remember, and yet there was only me sitting in my cramped seat, my body wracked with discomfort after such a long flight, the recycled air making my skin feel plastic, and then this. "How did we end up in the water?"

Ryan looked at me, stunned. "You don't remember?"

I shook my head.

"Maybe it's better that way."

Derek rose. "The plane crashed in the Amazon. At least that's what the map on my seat showed. You don't remember bracing yourself? The flight attendants freaking out?"

"She said no, Derek!" This from Viv.

Derek said, "The plane broke apart. Flooded. We were lucky to get out."

I didn't remember any of it. "How did I get out?"

"Same way we did," Derek said. "We were all sitting near each other. Near the exit rows. Threw on our life jackets or grabbed seat cushions and jumped in the water. A lot of people...." He paused. "A lot of people didn't." Derek looked at the dead adults. "They did, though." He spit near the dead bodies.

"What are you talking about?"

"You should've seen 'em claw over everyone. Trampled over people. They scratched and pushed their way out. There were no heroes on that plane. Not them, at least. They deserved to die."

Nico shot back, "No one *deserved* to die. No one."

"I don't know," Derek said. "Bet if you checked under their fingernails, you'd find human skin."

Ryan interrupted, "Anyone see Conlin?" We shook our heads. Pete Conlin was Ryan's best friend. "He was sitting right next to me. He was right there." Ryan peered out over the water, as if he could see Pete in the distance. "He was right next to me."

I don't remember what I did next. Maybe I cried. Maybe I fell on the ground. I receded back inside myself where nothing could hurt me. It didn't make sense. None of it made sense. Beyond the wreckage and bodies, we were in some kind of Garden of Eden, untouched by humans, as pristine as anything I'd ever seen, canopies of trees, and plants and flowers like colorful origami, a perfume of nature, and yet we'd fallen from the sky. I hunched over, shivering, saying to myself *I am safe, I am safe, I am safe.*

Our layers of clothes were so wet there was no point in wearing them. Derek was missing a shoe. Most of Nico's pants were ripped from the waist down. Viv's designer sweatpants clung to her body. Ryan fiddled with his remaining prosthetic leg, knocking sand loose from the joints and making sure it moved properly. Disjointed and detached from his body, it looked out of place, like the rest of this nightmare. With his jeans rolled up, I saw his stump covered in scar tissue.

Derek stood near the jungle's entrance, a quizzical look on his face, almost scientific. He didn't seem all that fazed, and even ran his hand over some of the trees, feeling their bark. I wondered what was wrong with him.

Molly sat on the shore, plopped down like a scoop of soft-serve ice cream, her head in her hands. She sat alone, and I felt bad for her, but she had earned the nickname Mean Molly for a reason. I got up anyway and approached her. Even as I asked it, I felt stupid. "Are you okay?"

She ignored me. Then she spoke. "I never wanted to come on this trip."

Molly didn't once look at me. She just kept staring ahead. I left her alone.

Viv, Nico and I formed a triangle on the ground. Viv and Nico leaned into each other, and Viv's crying went from a soft cry into heaves of despair. "I just want to go home. I just want to go home."

We didn't know it then, but the jungle was to become our home for far too long.

In the minutes that we sat or stood, there was just that moment, as if time had stopped altogether. Nico shook his silver watch, its face cracked, hands motionless. He sighed and slipped it back on. Then he took off one of his soaked tennis shoes and peeled off a wet sock. He reached inside the sock and pulled out a plastic baggie. The baggie was tightly wound and he unrolled it, revealing about an eighth of marijuana. Finding it dry, he smiled. "Small victories." Nico was a smart kid, on the National Honor Society, and some of the kids never understood how he got such good grades when he smoked so much pot.

Viv stopped crying, and asked, "You brought that on the plane? You could've been arrested."

Nico replied ruefully, "Maybe it would've been better if I was."

He pinched off a bud, intertwined with what looked like orange hairs, and offered it to me. I'd tried pot once or twice, but it made me feel paranoid. That's the last thing I needed. He offered the bud to Viv. She shook her head.

"You're going to eat it?"

He shrugged. "Can't smoke it."

"Nico, please…I need you. Don't."

He rubbed his nose, trying to move it from side to side, and grimaced. "I think it's broken. Hurts." Then he popped the bud into his mouth and swallowed, cringing. "Hurts a lot." Still feeling her judgmental gaze, he said, "Not now, Viv. Not now."

She looked away, too overwhelmed to argue.

This had happened. This had actually happened. Yet, the feeling of unreality permeated everything. I kept thinking any minute now a friendly tour guide would pop out from behind the overgrowth and ask, "Had enough?" Then he'd bring us to a concession stand and we'd find we were all in a theme park, one giant theme park—the latest in Disney's effort to bring the jungle to the masses.

No tour guide came.

Moments passed.

My fight-or-flight endorphins began to wane and my body suddenly felt very, very tired. My head throbbed, a remnant from slamming into the rocks.

Ryan stood, his one leg reattached, gripping a tree for balance. He was the school athlete and took to running track with custom blades. Some of the kids he picked on, including Derek, called him Darth Vader, "more machine than man, twisted and evil." But no one had the guts to say it to his face.

He rubbed his hands over his buzz cut. "Is everybody okay?" When we looked at him stunned, he added, "I meant, any injuries?"

Everyone seemed to be able to move their fingers and toes.

Derek said, "I say we go back up the river, that's where the search party will look first." He was normally an awkward kid at school, but he spoke with more authority now.

Ryan said, "Did you see the rapids we just went through? No way we're going back that way."

"I'm telling you, there'll be search parties. They'll be looking for us where the plane went down. It's that way." Derek pointed up the churning river. "The further we move, the harder it'll be for them to find us."

"You see those rock cliffs?" Ryan pointed to the side of the rapids we'd just come through. Jagged cliffs about three stories high flanked the river. "We're not going back." Looking the other direction, he said, "We can walk this." For as far as we could see, the land was flat, the river cooled to a normal current, and there seemed to be a mud path next to it.

Derek argued, "I actually know what I'm talking about."

"No one cares what you think. The river leads to the ocean, I know that much. There's gotta be a village along here somewhere."

I said, "Why can't we stay here?" Ignoring me was something Ryan and Derek could agree on. I added, "We might have injuries we don't even know about. Internal ones."

Ryan said, "All the more reason we need to find help."

Viv said, "I think Em's right. Why don't we stay here?"

Ryan snapped, "Because we have to *do* something. I'm not just gonna sit here and wait. I'm not just gonna hope. We need to move. We need to move down river. That's where I'm going."

Derek looked at the rest of us. "You're all just gonna sit there and listen to him?"

"Derek," I said, trying to calm him down. "Let's take a vote."

"Take a vote?"

Viv looked up. "Then go by yourself."

Derek scanned the group. "Okay. Let's vote. Who wants to come with me?" He raised his hand. No one else did. Defeat spread across his face. Out of sympathy, I raised my hand.

"Really, Em?" asked Viv.

I considered, looking at the determination on Ryan's face, and put my hand down. It was decided. We would head down the river towards the ocean. I hoped Ryan was right. Rather than trek off by himself, Derek stuck with the safety of the group. Peer pressure, it seemed, was as powerful in the jungle as it was in high school.

For the strangest reason, the poem by Robert Frost popped into my head. "The Road Not Taken."

> *Two roads diverged in a wood, and I—*
> *I took the one less traveled by,*
> *And that has made all the difference.*

We would take the road less traveled that was for sure. But whether it made all the difference, I would never know.

CHAPTER TWO

I've loved to read ever since I was a kid. Books have given me an escape from my own forgettable life. They've taken me to places I'll probably never see. They've introduced me to people and events and made me feel less alone. Words aren't just words; they're alchemy. But it's one thing to read and another to write. Writing, I'm finding, is an exorcism. I type on my laptop and it's torture. Remembering every detail is like ripping pieces of skin off my body where even the weight of air feels excruciating. Yet there is an underlying sense of relief to feel I am letting go. That's probably what my counselor wanted all along. For me to let go.

I wonder if I can. I wonder if I want to.

I will only tell this story once. It's too painful to ever do again.

There's a knock at the door. It slowly opens and it's Miranda Wert, Derek's mother. Miranda is usually so put together. Not today. She's without makeup and her face is hidden by dark sunglasses. Her clothes weigh her down and her normally straight hair is wavy, which is what I assume is its natural state. There's a frailness about her, as if a strong gust might send her to the floor. She stands in the doorway, her gaze lost on me, and I wonder if she's picturing her son alive instead of me.

It's not the same, but I can't imagine what it would be like to lose my mom. We don't have the best of relationships, but she's all I have.

Mrs. Wert stands, hesitating, her hand on the doorknob as if waiting for me to invite her in.

"Mrs. Wert?"

Her dark sunglasses face me. "Emily." Her voice sounds far away.

"Come in."

She lingers near the door. "I didn't know if this was a good time…."

"It's fine."

"I can always come back."

Now that she's here, it's like she wants to leave. "Now's fine, really."

She walks into the room and stops a few feet from my bed. Her mouth opens to speak, and then shuts. Her head drops. "I'm sorry," she sighs. "I didn't even bring flowers."

"It's okay."

She looks around the room as if getting her bearings. "How are you feeling?"

"Not sure. They say I'm getting better. Doesn't feel like it, though."

"I don't know what I'm doing here…."

"Please stay."

She sits down and we share an awkward silence. She fidgets, absentmindedly picking at her cuticles. They're raw and red. I finally say, "I'm sorry about your son." I mentally cringe. Saying nothing would be better.

"No one told me what happened," she says. "I mean, they did in general terms. The plane crashed due to mechanical failure. You were the only survivor. But no one told me what happened to my son. What really happened."

"The plane crashed from mechanical failure?"

"No one told you?"

I shake my head. It's weird. Knowing why the plane went down doesn't seem all that important. It certainly doesn't fix anything.

Miranda says, "I kept up on the news for a while and then couldn't. I haven't been outside…." She seems to be mentally counting the days. "Since the funeral."

"I'm sorry I couldn't come." What a stupid thing to say. Trying to say something concrete, I say, "I know a few lawyers have already been in contact with my mom."

"Lawyers," she says more to herself. "No amount of money will bring back my son." She fixes her gaze on me. "Can you tell me what happened?"

Anything to make her feel better.

I tell her how we journeyed into the jungle, living off Derek's knowledge, eating grubs and drinking water. "All the years you went camping as a family kept us going for quite a while."

A small smile rests on her lips. "I always hated camping." She gets out of her chair and goes to the window with its closed blinds. "Do you want these open?"

"No," I say. "I like them closed."

She looks at me oddly, her hand on the circular rod, and lets go. She crosses back to the chair and takes her glasses off. Her eyes are tired and ragged. I thought in the jungle we looked beaten, but Miranda is the definition of broken. She asks, her voice flat, "How did he die?"

I hesitate. "Are you sure?"

She says, simply, "Yes."

The room suddenly feels too small and even though the air conditioning is on, I'm uncomfortably warm.

"He was my baby, my little boy…."

"I'll tell you," I say. "I'll tell you what you want to know." I gather my thoughts and begin. "After so many days, I don't even remember, we were only alive because of him. His skill at hunting, picking out which food was edible or not. Without him, I wouldn't be here."

Miranda pinches the bridge above her nose, and there are tears in her eyes.

"Would you like me to stop?"

"Go on," she says. "Please."

"We were out fishing. Derek had a spear and sometimes he'd spearfish. I don't know how he was able to do it. He let me try a few times, and I always missed. The fish always seemed to see me coming, no matter how fast I was. But Derek, he was a pro. He'd hold the spear right over the water. He knew at just what angle to jab 'em…we never did find a way to make a fire. But I know if we were there long enough, he would have."

Mrs. Wert listens quietly.

"Derek thrived out there. He could take care of himself." I take a breath and continue. "The day he died, we were out near the river. I see a spot across the way where we haven't been. There's a whole patch of mushrooms. So we cross. I thought it was just going to go up to our waist, but suddenly, it drops. The water was deep and there was a current. Me and Molly fall in and…."

I stop.

"I'm sorry, Emily. I know this is hard for you."

That only makes me feel worse—that she's worried how I feel.

"You have to understand, we were so tired. I couldn't walk more than, I don't know, it felt like only yards, without being exhausted. We were only eating enough to keep us from starving, so when we fell into the water…we had no strength."

"You don't have to explain."

"We were so weak, the water was taking us. And…." I try not to cry. "I wanted to die, Mrs. Wert. I was so tired. We weren't living. We were just *there*. I thought we were forgotten, stuck, forever. In that moment, I gave up. I let go. I was saying goodbye when all of a sudden, I felt Derek's arms around me, and he's swimming, telling me it's going to be okay, to just hold on, he's got me. He swam with me, I don't know how, carrying me across the river and then he got me on shore. He rescued me. He literally saved my life."

"As I'm lying there, catching my breath, he goes back in. Molly was still in trouble. The current was taking her and she was getting farther and farther away. I knew he was tired. I said his name. I don't think he heard me. Derek swam but when he got to her, she panicked. She was flailing. Derek tried to calm her down, but she was so scared. He held onto her even though she didn't know what she was doing…."

I cry and I see that Miranda is crying.

"They drowned, Mrs. Wert. They hit some rocks, and they went face down. He never came back out. I don't think he was in any pain."

The only sound in the room is us. Mrs. Wert covers her face with her hands and she's trembling. I hear her muffled sobs.

"I won't lie, Mrs. Wert. While we were there we did things to survive. Things we would regret. But at the end, when it counted, your son was a hero."

Miranda reaches her hand to mine and holds on tight. "Thank you, Emily. Thank you so much." We stay this way for minutes, her hand grasping mine in little pulses. Then she stands up and wipes her tears. "I didn't want to cry."

"I know it's not much, Mrs. Wert."

"It's everything." She places her sunglasses back on and gathers herself. She wipes her clothes as if she's spilled crumbs on them. "He was an only child, you know? Sometimes I wonder what that makes me now."

"His mother."

She has the faintest of smiles. "I know he's not here. But I'm glad you are, Emily. When this is all over, don't be a stranger, okay?"

"I promise," I lie. If we ever met, she'd see the ghost of her son next to me. I wouldn't inflict that pain on her. "Thanks for coming, Mrs. Wert."

She's at the door and straightens herself, mentally making herself presentable before she opens it. She turns to me. "Please, call me Miranda."

"Miranda."

Then she's gone.

It's a nice story. A nice story for a mother to hear, but unfortunately not true. That's not the real story at all. The real story is much more complicated.

We trekked along the river, its water brown and muddy, staying close to the shore. If we got lucky, maybe we'd see a boat. No one said anything, all of us shaken in disbelief and shock. My brain seemed to go slack, as if it simply overloaded and switched off.

Ryan had found a knobby stick and used it as a crutch. He limped along and if we survived I knew exactly how he'd look as an old man. It was slow going. All around it smelled of wet earth and dirt.

Next to us the forest sang. It was a cacophony of noise; insects buzzing, birds squawking, frogs croaking, and in the distance, did I hear *howling*?

Nico perked up at the sound, his eyes saucer wide. Stoned, he said, "This is crazy. We're like, *in the jungle*. Seriously, listen to that…." He tilted his head, following the sounds. "It's, like, stereophonic."

Though I envied his sense of wonder, I hoped in his altered state he would keep his mouth shut. I didn't want him to say something he shouldn't.

After a time, the shoreline grew thinner, forcing us to the river's edge until up ahead the path disappeared altogether. It was either swim or veer into the jungle.

No one said they were scared, but it was obvious. At least here you could see. Who knew what lay behind the wall of green? But there was no choice.

Entering the rainforest was like passing through a green curtain into a massive haunted room. It was as claustrophobic as I feared. We could only see a few feet in front of us, like a bank of fog, except it was trees and vines: trees that soared well into the sky, vines that grew at impossible angles and thick waxy leaves that blotted out the sun.

Thin shafts of light pierced through the canopy of trees, and sunlight barely touched bottom. The air was humid and sticky, as though we walked through gelatinous water. The temperature dropped by ten degrees and my clothes chafed against my skin, soon to go raw if I didn't get dry.

I didn't like it. Not at all.

If we were slow going before, we were now reduced to a crawl. The growth was thick, sometimes up to our knees, and tangles of branches caught on our legs as if the jungle was actively trying to trip us. In some places we couldn't see the jungle floor. The ground itself wasn't firm, but spongy, like a carpet of memory foam mattresses.

All was alien, a blast of green and brown, a soundscape of nature turned up to ten, and a whole swath of dense monotony. One tree so like another, it's as if we were moving in place.

Viv's breathing started to go shallow. She was fighting a panic attack. Nico stopped and took her in his arms. "Viv, it's okay. Look at me. Look in my eyes."

"The jungle," she stammered, "it's closing in on us."

"It's not, Viv. It's not. We'll be okay."

Viv fought the hysteria rising in her voice. "We're gonna die, we're gonna die…." She was hyperventilating, and I was angry that she brought my own fear—my own doubts—to the surface. "We're gonna die out here. No one will ever know what happened to us."

Molly stepped up to Viv and sharply slapped her in the face. We all stopped. This never would've happened back at school.

Nico pushed Molly away. "The hell you do that for?"

Molly nodded toward Viv. "She seems fine now."

Sure enough, Viv did. The slap took the fear out of her and replaced it with anger.

In P.E. class, a volleyball smacked against my head. I hated volleyball. I hated track. I hated P.E. To me it was a wasted hour that I could have spent sleeping in, reading the latest John Green, or doing a million other things than mandated exercise. The only thing I liked was seeing how the unisex gym shorts and shirts made all the girls look the same, even the most endowed of us. In gym class, no one looked good. No one stood out. It was fashion communism.

P.E. was the only class I shared with Molly Higgins. She was a year older than me, a Senior, and while I don't like judging people or being critical about appearances (I'm well aware of my own issues), there's no denying that she's, well, big. But there were a lot of big people in high school. What made Molly stand out was her face. With a permanent frown and exaggerated bone structure, she looked like an angry bull. It says something about her that she earned the nickname Mean Molly over Fat Molly. I never saw anyone pick on her. Not even in whispers. I'd heard that in grade school she beat up boys and smacked around girls. The reputation stuck.

One time after gym class, we went into the locker room. Molly stood across from me, and I watched her change. She took off her shirt and I saw the rolls of fat and I felt a stab of pity. It must be very hard to be Molly Higgins. Then she caught me staring.

She said, "Think you're better than me?"

"No."

"Then what? You like girls?"

"No," I sputtered.

"Then stop staring."

"I'm sorry."

"That's right," she said. "You *are* sorry."

We moved like numb marionettes moving for the sake of moving, in a line, one behind the other. It was the easiest way to travel. Not side-by-side but single file, as if moving through a tunnel. Suddenly, Molly stopped, breathing in short bursts. I thought she might be having a heart attack.

Ryan said, "We have to keep moving."

"I can't."

We stopped, each privately grateful for the break, and grateful we weren't the cause. One minute became two and two became three. Ryan prodded her. "C'mon, Molly."

"Don't touch me!"

"Molly." Not a question: a statement, a command.

"I'm tired. I'm hungry. I didn't even want to take this trip."

Ryan looked at her coldly. "If you don't get up and start moving, I will leave you where you are. *We* will leave you where you are. Is that what you want?"

"I'm tired."

"We're all tired!" He took a breath and rubbed his face. She was immovable and he squatted right in front of her, gently lifting her face so that they were eye-to-eye. "Doesn't matter what your body is telling you. Your body is lying. It's lazy. But *you're* not. You can get up. You can do extraordinary things. If I can do it, you can, too. You can do so much more than you think."

"I can't."

"You can. You will. Say it after me. I can, I will."

She said quietly, "I'm pregnant…."

We were stunned.

Ryan said, "What? Why didn't you say anything?"

"Isn't it obvious?" She looked away in shame. "I was scared. Embarrassed. I should've known better."

Having a baby at her age was going to be a life-changer. No matter our past, I felt sympathetic. I couldn't imagine becoming a mother. Not for a long time.

Derek asked, "Who's the father?" I wondered the same thing. I hadn't seen her around with anyone. Maybe it was someone from a different school.

Viv said, "Does it matter?"

He shrugged. "Just curious."

We waited for Molly to catch her breath. I feared if we didn't move soon, our bodies would turn to stone. After a time—too much time—we began walking again and made our way parallel with the river, towards the ocean and hopefully a village.

My tongue seemed heavy, an appendage that didn't belong. I tried to remember if we could drink river water, whether it was fresh water or salt, or if it didn't matter because of all the bacteria and parasites that polluted it. Probably any water was drinkable with iodine or boiling, but we had no fire, no iodine and no canteen—no god damn nothing.

I admit the thought of drinking my own urine crossed my mind. I'd seen it done on some Discovery survival show and what had disgusted me then suddenly seemed necessary. But without a bowl or glass I wasn't even sure it was possible. I was getting desperate enough to drink blood. Kill an animal and gorge on it like some kind of maniac. Anything but die of thirst.

Derek seemed to read my mind. He stopped near a big brown puddle of stagnant water and got on his hands and knees. About two feet from the puddle, he began digging a hole.

Ryan stopped, unsure of what was happening.

Once the hole was about a foot deep, Derek stopped and sat back on his ankles. Water slowly filtered into the hole, rising from the bottom up. The group circled around him.

"Now what?" Ryan asked.

"We wait," Derek said.

"For what?" I asked.

"The water to filter out and let the dirt settle."

We continued to stare at this most basic of things—water seeping into a hole and after what seemed like an eternity, the hole was filled.

The water was still brown. Molly said, "Looks gross."

"Better than dying." Derek was about to place his face in the water when he stopped. He took a gentlemanly pose, offering the first drink to Molly. She reluctantly obliged and lapped it up like a dog.

I fought the urge to push them all aside and submerge my face, and looking at them, felt they were thinking the same.

Derek went next, followed by Nico and Viv.

Nico asked him, "Where'd you learn to do that?"

Derek looked pointedly at Ryan. "Boy Scouts."

I could tell Ryan's pride wanted him to deny the water, but his thirst was too much. Letting his stick drop, he moved to the hole and hopped over. As he took a drink, Derek said, "Betcha don't think Scouts are such fags now, do you?"

Ryan finished and wiped his hand across his face. He held Derek's gaze and then got back up, retrieving his stick while I took the last drink. The water was surprisingly cool. To me it tasted like champagne. I was surprised that something so elemental lifted my spirits. This was my Fountain of Youth. We were going to be all right. We would survive. We would be okay.

I was wrong.

CHAPTER THREE

Just because I attended Riverdale Academy High, one of the premiere private high schools in Los Angeles, it didn't mean I was privileged. Take the parking lot, for example. Lost among the fleet of BMWs, Mercedes and even cars that looked like they could fly when their doors opened, sat my used, dented Honda. I nicknamed it Harriet. No reason. Every morning started with a gentle pat on the dashboard and a soothing *c'mon, Harriet.* She never failed and carried me within the triangle that was my life: home, school, and work.

As a scholarship student, I worked part-time everyday after school at Burger King, home of the Whopper, minimum wage, and a large serving of humble pie. No extra-curricular activities for me. Work and study were my two basic food groups.

Derek worked with me, not that he needed money. His parents forced him to work in order to understand the ins and outs of business from the ground up. While I worked in the back, he worked the cash register and was the face customers saw, especially school kids.

Unfortunately, kids from our school.

I never really knew Ryan before now. He seemed like one of those people who made decisions easily, as if he was born fully formed, fully adult. One time he came in with his girlfriend-of-the-moment. Her father ran a movie studio and there was talk that he'd buy Ryan's life-rights for a feel-good-kid-faces-adversity-and-does-well kind of story. Never materialized.

Derek asked, his face emanating grease, "May I take your order?"

Ryan ordered a combo meal. His girlfriend turned to Ryan, and she whispered something while giggling and pointing at Derek's face.

Derek kept calm, seemingly used to it. But sometimes I caught him looking in the mirror, rubbing his palm over his cratered face and cringing. I could relate, as I often found myself looking in the mirror at home, unhappy with the size of my breasts or the shape of my body.

"Seriously," she said, "he's, like, a walking oil slick."

I watched helplessly from behind the grill. I hated it. Not because of any love for Derek, but anyone who wore the polyester hat like I did was okay in my book. Messing with him was like messing with me.

Ryan said, to his credit and my surprise, "Just order, will you?"

She turned to Derek. "I'm not trying to be mean, but you should see a dermatologist. They can fix that, you know. If your parents don't, that's like, *abuse*." She paused to take in the menu. "I'll take a burger. No onions."

I pictured her sticking her finger down her throat and bringing it back up later.

Derek asked, "Anything to drink with that?"

"Just water."

No, I didn't spit in her food. That's gross. But I did wipe her bun on the bottom of my shoe.

The heat was oppressive. We were swimming in air, rather than walking through it. I had a constant sheen of moisture on my skin. To distract myself, I pictured wearing a fedora, wielding a whip and machete, and facing any situation with humor like a female Indiana Jones. It was the only way to pretend this was something adventurous. I told myself we weren't running from a plane crash; we were running to an Indian tribe who would feed us, save us, and maybe offer us an ancient gold relic with magical powers. Like the power of going home. I lost myself in this mini-fantasy until I got sick of almost tripping, swatting away bugs, and fighting the throb of a headache.

Seemingly moving in place from one green prison cell to another was making me dizzy. I fought the sensation of nausea, looking up in the sky to get a point of reference. The rainforest was like a real-life myth: the Minotaur's labyrinth colored in lime.

Inspired, I said, "Hey." The formation stopped. "We should leave a mark. A trail. Let rescuers know we've been here."

Nico asked, "With what?"

"I don't know." Sensing it was a good idea, everyone searched their pockets and found nothing. Then I noticed my cross-body bag. I opened the zipper. Rummaging inside, I found my wallet, cell phone—

I'd forgotten it was there! Even though it was soaked, I pressed the power button and in crazy desperation hoped it would work.

Please, please, please.

"You got your phone?" This from Ryan.

I waited and waited, my hope soaring and soaring, only to crash.

I felt so stupid for allowing myself to believe.

Ryan said, "Throw it here."

We watched as he tried the button over and over, a holy grail that wasn't holy anymore. Frustrated, he swore and whipped the phone into the jungle.

Seconds passed and Nico asked, "Any of you carry lipstick?"

Viv wore makeup. She never left the house without it, but she didn't have her purse. Molly and I went natural.

I looked again in my cross-body bag and pulled out a book. It was small and the pages were wet, the edges curled. It was from my English teacher, Mr. DeKoning. He'd self-published a book of poems.

He'd given me the book and encouraged me to explore writing. He said, "I thought you might like it." He'd even signed it *To Emily, my favorite student.*

I opened the book, took a page, and ripped it out. It was a poem entitled *Longing For What Never Came.* I hesitated. This had been a gift, an inspiration. The page lay in my hand, an artifact from the past. I approached a tree and silently said thank you to my teacher and then pierced the page with a branch. "This should work." The poem hung on the tree. I knew the pages would dissolve in the moisture before too long; I only hoped we were rescued before that happened. Just as Theseus had left string in the Minotaur's labyrinth in order to escape, so did I. Page by page, branch by branch, I left little signposts of paper in our wake.

The café was dark. A barista with a handlebar mustache gave us our lattes. Hipsters flitted to and fro, socializing among themselves. A lone microphone stood near the back. Viv turned to me. "So, we're here on a Wednesday night for…caffeine?"

"Wait, you'll see."

We took a seat away from the ad hoc stage—a tiny wooden plank—and sipped our drinks. I felt alive and excited, and couldn't tell if it was the caffeine or the thrill of coming here. After a few minutes, a balding man with suspenders came to the microphone, cleared his throat and thanked the sprinkling of audience members for coming to tonight's poetry reading.

Viv's eyebrows leapt up. "You brought us here for poetry?"

"C'mon, give it a chance. It won't be that bad."

"Em, it's poetry," as if that said it all. She checked her phone and engaged in a text conversation I wasn't privy to. She asked, "Why couldn't I have brought Nico?"

"I don't know, Viv. I want a girls night every once in a while."

The first speaker must've been an alcoholic because he spoke lovingly about his affair with a beer bottle, and how after they broke up he smashed the bottle, only to try and piece it back together like Humpty-Dumpty. The second guy did some mash-up of words talking so fast I couldn't tell what the point was other than a kind of spoken Jackson Pollack painting.

Then the balding man introduced the next speaker, as simply, Johannes. I saw him rise from the audience. He looked over the scattered crowd, his eyes finding mine, surprise on his face.

"Hey," Viv whispered. "It's Mr. DeKoning."

Mr. DeKoning seemed nervous, so much different than how he stood in front of the classroom. In class, he exuded a youthful confidence. He was the kind of teacher everybody wants: funny, almost our age (well, 24, but only a few years out of college), with an interesting history: he was first-generation Dutch, which brought an avalanche of jokes and comments about Amsterdam's red light district. Of course he was handsome, but not in that cocky, bad-boy way. He was sensitive and loved literature. He held a piece of paper in his hands, and the page slightly shook from his nervousness. I found it endearing.

"This is titled *Longing For What Never Came*." His nervousness disappeared as he spoke, less words and more emotion translated into air.

I listened and felt I was seeing into his soul.

"He's good," Viv whispered.

He was speaking to me, as if the words were written for me. About me.

As he finished, he'd mesmerized the whole audience, and I so wished I'd recorded it on my cell phone. It was seriously one of those things that would've gone viral. The audience gave a hearty applause.

I watched as he sat down, alone. No girlfriend, no posse of supporters. No fellow teachers.

Viv and I stayed for the rest, but the other speakers were forgettable. The balding man closed out the event, our coffees were empty, and I told Viv I was going to say hi to him.

"Ask him for his autograph," she teased.

As I approached him, a wave of pleasant anticipation filled me. "Hi," I said.

"Hi. Didn't expect anyone would show."

"Why not? You invited the whole class." I couldn't tell if he was depressed by the lack of student participation or relieved.

"I kinda knew in the back of my head no one would come. Poetry's poetry, you know? Hard to get people excited by it."

"Um," I said, pointing at myself. "Hello?" I had to admit I came because I was probably a teacher's pet, but there was no denying my curiosity about him.

Around us, the café started to empty. "I appreciate it. I really do."

"Was this your first time?"

"It was," and he laughed. "Could you tell?"

"Not at all."

"I purposely invited people, otherwise I might've bailed. Forced me to show up."

Talking to him felt like talking to…not a teacher. But a normal guy. "I loved it. Your poem, I mean. Definite A+."

"Really?"

"Yeah, it's way better than the stuff we read in class." I quickly added, "Nothing against your assignments."

"I doubt T.S Eliot and Maya Angelou would feel the same."

"No, really. I feel like I saw a side of you that you keep hidden. And maybe you shouldn't…'cause it's nice. That side." I blushed. "Sorry if I just got corny on you."

"Not at all." He looked at me differently. I could feel the shift. "Thanks, Emily. It means a lot. Now you can see if I'm practicing what I teach. Or if I'm just a total BSer." In class he'd always called us by our last names. Like Ms. Duran.

I returned the salutation. "See you in class, Johannes." I walked away, feeling his eyes on me and I felt…connected somehow. As if I just met the missing piece of the puzzle that was me.

In the car on the way home, Viv said, "So that's why we went there." She playfully sang the kissing song: "*First comes love, then comes marriage, then comes a baby in a baby carriage!*"

"It's nothing like that, Viv. He's, like, old."

"He's cute, isn't he?"

"Very cute," I agreed. "But not my type."

"Liar."

That night, I tossed and turned in my bed, feeling a heat within me I'd never felt before. I was crushing hard—on a teacher, no less. Not that it would go anywhere. Of course it would never go anywhere. Why couldn't I just date someone my own age? I'd tried, but they were *boys*. They talked about getting drunk and told jokes stolen from the internet; nothing they ever did was original, as if they were trying on different personas to see which one would stick. Boys my age didn't interest me. But Johannes DeKoning did, with his ever-so-slight Dutch accent and his Dutch-boy blonde hair and his professorial knowledge of literature. He was a man, a man of the world, and I was eager to learn.

Nothing would come of it, that was certain. Nothing at all.

We heard the river, its current resonating deep and wide. *The river leads to the ocean*, that's what Ryan had said. *There has to be a village nearby.* We veered towards it, stepping out of the overgrowth. A group of butterflies fluttered across the river, big and bright, and I felt they were a good omen.

Ryan stopped first. Then the rest of us.

Bodies littered the river, caught in the rocks.

Not people, not any longer: bodies.

Bodies from the wreckage. Thirty, maybe forty or more. I didn't count. I wouldn't; they weren't objects to be counted.

They must've floated downstream as the plane flooded and got caught in the river's eddy. They bobbed in the water. On TV, it always looks as if dead people are merely like live ones, just not moving. As if life itself had evaporated from them leaving a calm husk in its place. This was real life, and they were dead: faces tinted blue, the skin no longer skin, but waxy, and the eyes dark orbs. Flies flecked over them, emerging from open mouths. How odd not to see someone blink.

Molly pointed into the water. Her voice was flat. "Him. I sat next to him. He told me his name, but I don't remember it. He hogged my armrest."

Pieces of wreckage floated on the water, bits of suitcases, a backpack or two, air sickness bags. I saw a teddy bear and I wanted to cry.

Then I saw movement.

The bodies weren't bobbing because of the current. They were bobbing because of something underneath. The bodies rose up and down in minuscule beats, pulled down, and then allowed to rise. Little concentric circles rippled from their herky-jerky spasms.

Under them the water turned red.

This. Can't. Be.

This was nature at work. Meat was in the water. The piranhas were having a feast.

Repulsed and hysterical, I rushed into the water, the water up to my ankles, and I screamed, "Leave them alone! Leave them alone!" I tried to shoo them away when I felt Nico's arms around me. He picked me up and carried me out of the water and the next thing I knew I was on shore.

"Don't ever do that!" He took my face in his hands. "You can't save them. You can't stop it." He released me and I looked past him.

The water churned like miniature blenders, and if I watched closely I could see the remnants of more passengers. Seat cushions and clothes I thought had come loose from suitcases: they hadn't come from suitcases. The torn jeans, the ripped shirts, they were all that were left.

I wanted to be sick, but nothing came up. Just the taste of bile. I couldn't even cry; I was too dehydrated. How messed up is that? To want to cry only to have your body deny you.

Viv sat next to me, her arm around my back and she leaned her head on my shoulder. "Just look away, Emily. There's nothing there."

"But there is."

She gently turned my head away. "What kind of flower is that?"

I knew what she was trying to do, distract me, but I couldn't help but turn back and stare. "It's random, Viv. It's all so *random*. Why did we live and they didn't? Why did we make it on shore and no one else did? Why were we special?"

"I don't know, Emily."

"I don't know, either."

Viv looked me in the eye. "Do you wish you were them?"

"No."

"Then look away."

I was about to when Derek ran into the water. I thought it was the most ridiculous way to commit suicide. I thought of all the taunts he'd gotten at school; how kids took his last name "Wert," and chanted "Wart! Wart!

Wart!"; how with gangly steps that only highlighted his lanky frame, he was trying to end it all with some story that would make him infamous—"the guy who got eaten by piranha."

I shouted, "Stop!"

No one tried to save him like Nico had saved me.

But Derek wasn't trying to commit suicide. He splashed out of the water almost as fast as he'd gotten in. Wet up to his knees, he carried a piece of metal. I couldn't tell if it was a piece of the plane's wing or what, but it was triangular. He held it in his hand, about two feet in length, and he ran his finger over the edge, satisfied it was sharp.

Ryan mocked him. "What the fuck, fucktard?"

Derek said, "You might want to rephrase that. I'm the one with a hatchet." To prove his point, with a few solid *whacks* he cut a vine from off a tree.

"You never cease to amaze me with your weirdness."

"What's weird about me getting a tool? You understand how I just helped you? Helped all of us?"

"Look at what you did to get it."

Derek turned to Ryan. "You know what's weird? I keep thinking, like a bad habit, your football friends are gonna have your back. Like you and Conlin. That he's hiding behind some tree, just waiting for me to look the other way and then boom! Push me to the ground. Or knock shit out of my hands. Or if he's feeling really generous, pretend to rape me. That's what you and he liked to do. For 'fun', right?" He turned the metal piece in his hands. "Then it hit me. He isn't here. He isn't coming. He won't be coming. Your asshole friend Pete Conlin is never coming." He held the metal like a knife. "What do you say to that, *fucktard*?"

Ryan stood, taking in this turn of events, and I couldn't tell what was written on his face. Fear? Karma?

Nico said, "Why don't we all just calm down. No one's thinking straight."

Something changed in Ryan's face and he stepped forward, crutch and all, and knocked the metal piece from Derek's hand. It fell to the ground. Derek's face fell with it.

"Don't ever mention my friend again. Not from your mouth."

Derek stood a moment, considering his options. He said defiantly, "Pete. Conlin."

"Derek," I said, imploring. "Stop." I didn't want to see him get hurt. I didn't want to see a fight. Not after everything we'd been through.

But it was Derek who wouldn't back down. "Enough of the threats. If you want to beat me up so bad, do it. There's no principal to get in the way. No fear of getting kicked out of school."

Ryan shook his head and did nothing. "You're not worth it, Wart."

Derek said, "Thought so."

Ryan hopped back to the front of the group. "Let's keep going. Those bodies are only gonna attract more wildlife."

We didn't stick around to see if he was right.

The sun began to set, and it created a blanket of rose in the sky. At least some things were the same no matter where you were.

"We'd better make a shelter," said Derek. "Once the sun goes down, it'll be dark. And I mean *dark*."

Viv spoke up. "Shelter?" The implication was clear. We thought we'd be in the jungle only a few hours at most before being rescued.

Derek said, "You see any planes? Helicopters? Flares?"

We hadn't. We were on our own.

I kept trying to convince myself we were going to be all right. I kept failing.

Nico sat near the base of a gnarled tree, its trunk nearly ten feet thick, surrounded by a tangle of roots. "I think I'll just sit here." Ryan and Viv followed Nico's lead.

"I wouldn't do that. You'll be covered by bugs come morning."

Scared of the idea, Viv stood up. So did Nico. Ryan stayed put.

I asked Derek, "What do you need?"

He scanned the area, his eyes settling on tall stalks of bamboo, thick and round. "Help me cut this stuff."

For the next half hour, we helped him hold bamboo as he cut it with his makeshift hatchet. He cut four posts and rammed them vertically in the ground, the soft mud giving way easily, each about a foot high, which made a base. Then he placed two longer pieces of bamboo on them. From there, he placed cross pieces. Suddenly, from nothing he had created a bedframe. Though he explained as he went along using words like "bamboo nodes" and "V-grooves," I couldn't follow it all. I was just impressed that here in the jungle was the closest thing to civilization—a bed—that I'd seen.

Finally, he added layers of bamboo across the whole thing and created a kind of mattress. Satisfied with his work, he lay back on it and theatrically crisscrossed his legs and placed his arms behind his head. He sighed deeply. "Home, sweet home."

After a moment he got up. "Actually, Molly, this one's for you."

"Really?"

He nodded. Molly sat on the bed, made herself comfortable and watched us. Maybe being pregnant had its perks.

Viv asked, "What if they don't come?"

Nico replied, moving his dark mop of hair out of his eyes, "They'll come."

"What if they don't?"

More insistent this time, Nico said, "They'll come."

She looked up at the sky, or what she could see of it. "Then why aren't they here?"

The question went unanswered until she repeated it.

"Because," Ryan said, as if the answer was obvious, "it's the Amazon, not America."

The sun seemed to set in time with our falling hopes.

Derek was right: the dark wasn't just lack of light; it was a presence—a suffocating presence. The sounds that had emanated from behind the wall of green during the day, the drone of crickets and insects, seemed louder. Closer. Ominous.

There were a total of five thin beds, one for each of us, save Ryan. He rested against a tree and closed his eyes.

I didn't want to sleep alone, so I snuck next to Viv, feeling her warmth.

She whispered, "Tell me a story. You're good with stories."

The only thing I knew by heart was a stanza by Henry David Thoreau. It was "Friendship," and I whispered to her:

Two sturdy oaks I mean, which side by side
Withstand the winter's storm,
And spite of wind and tide,
Grow up the meadow's pride,
For both are strong

Above they barely touch, but undermined
Down to their deepest source,
Admiring you shall find
Their roots are intertwined
Insep'rably.

Viv was sound asleep.

As I lay snuggled next to her, I took a deep breath. While the air was oppressive during the day, at night it cooled. It was as fresh and pure as I have ever breathed. In a day filled with horrors, the air provided the one and only sense of pleasure.

Looking up, I saw the moon through the canopy. I wondered if my mother was seeing the same view from back home. Did my mother know about the crash yet? Or was she living in a comfortable haze of normalcy?

I hoped so. Enjoy those moments, mother. Someone should.

I covered my face in the folds of my shirt to avoid the buzzing of mosquitoes and closed my eyes. The jungle screamed in protest.

CHAPTER FOUR

"Emily...." It's my mother's voice. She gently shakes me and I open my eyes. She hovers over me in the hospital room, her face inches from mine. I can smell the lingering scent of menthol cigarettes in her hair, on her breath, a combination of mint and smoke. She must have started smoking again.

"You were having a nightmare."

I didn't remember it. "What was I saying this time?"

"The same thing.... 'Viv, come back.'"

"I'll be okay, mom."

I see her glance down at the sheets, eyes filled with concern, and she presses her hand against the mattress. I've wet my bed again. I'm ashamed to admit, but in the jungle I didn't get up at night to go to the bathroom. I was too scared. So I held it until I couldn't hold it any longer.

"Should I call a nurse?"

I shake my head. I just want to sleep. In the grand scheme of things, a wet bedspread is nothing. Losing a best friend is another altogether.

I first met Vivian Liu on a sunny summer day under the bleachers at a local park. I was stretched out, legs in front of me, my body resting against a beam, reading. Behind me, kids shrieked, joining the music of whistles and drifting voices, but as I turned the pages, the world around me fell away.

It was the summer after seventh grade, and my mother, worried that I hadn't lost my baby fat or scared at my blindingly pale skin, figured signing me up for the local soccer team would give me a dose of athleticism I wanted no part of. That soccer didn't interest me didn't seem to matter. "Getting outside will do you good," she'd said. I had no intention of chasing after a ball while trying to avoid getting kicked in the shins. But being a dutiful daughter, I dressed the part, gym bag in hand, and as soon as she dropped me off, I'd wander over to the bleachers. Hidden in my bag was a book, and I proceeded to read until she picked me up later in the afternoon. I did that every time. By the end of the summer, still pale, she told me to stop wearing so much sunscreen.

"What're you reading?"

I looked up to see a girl I'd never seen before standing in front of me. She seemed about my age, dark hair falling to her shoulders like silk, with naturally tanned skin. She, too, wore a girls' soccer uniform, but she wasn't from my team. Her tone wasn't accusatory, just curious.

"It's *Beowulf*."

Her eyes knitted together. "Are you in summer school or something?"

"No. Just reading for fun." I could see the incomprehension on her face, as if I'd told her I was from the moon, so I dog-eared the book and handed it to her. "It's a graphic novel, see?"

"Like a comic book?"

Not wanting to explain the difference, I said, "Kind of. It's about a monster, Grendel." I watched as the girl turned the pages, genuinely interested in the blocks of art like a movie captured in print. "There. And he attacks this great hall. But, to me he's not really a monster, 'cause his mother is a dragon. If you flip forward...." She did. "Yeah, her."

"Cool," the girl said.

"And that's why Grendel is the way he is. At least, that's what I think."

"So, you just come out here and read?"

I nodded. "Supposed to play soccer, but I ditch."

"You do?" She laughed. "Really? I didn't think that was possible. I mean, of course it is. I want to every day, but I just never…." She blew a strand of hair out of her face. "Soccer's not even about having fun. My mom and dad just want me to be able to say that I did it."

"Why?"

"Colleges love extra-curriculars. As if I care."

I couldn't tell if I was jealous that her parents were pushing her towards a goal, or relieved that my mother wasn't. "Aren't you supposed to be playing now?"

"Can I tell you a secret?" She whispered. "I. Hate. Soccer. With. A. Passion."

This time I laughed. "I thought it was just me."

"Getting all sweaty. Running around, banging into each other. And some of those girls? They're *into* it. Like, they'll scratch your eyes out. They're like that dragon. And the coach? You should see him. He's Stacey's father—she's a girl on my team. So annoying. Both of them. But you'd think coaching was his reason to live. I'm like, it's only soccer! There's more important things, you know. Like keeping my skin nice. Look at this." She pointed to a scab along her calf. "Some girl did this on purpose."

"She did?" I was even happier now to have ditched.

"It's like being with animals. They're *feral*. And these." There were splotches of bruises up and down her shoulder and arm. "Surprised I'm not dead yet. I took a bathroom break. Didn't really have to go, just had to get away." She paused and looked over at the field and then back at me. "Mind if I stay with you a while?"

"Are you gonna get in trouble? For being late?"

"What are they gonna do? Kick me off the team?" She put her hands in prayer position. "Please, please, please!"

I patted the ground next to me, inviting her to sit.

She plopped down. "I'm Viv, by the way."

"Emily."

She still held the book in her hands. "Can I borrow this sometime?"

"Sure," I said. "I've got a ton of others."

That's how I spent my summer. Meeting Viv at the bleachers. Sometimes we'd read, other times we'd walk around. But mainly we just talked. Hours and hours and hours, from topics stupid to serious. We were very different, I would learn. She came from money; she lived in a different neighborhood with big homes and better yards; and worse, she went to a different junior high.

Yet, we became inseparable.

That summer we each earned the title Best Friend.

Later, when Viv went to Riverdale Academy, I made it my mission to go there too. My mother may take credit for it, but it was always my idea. It wasn't the educational opportunities, though that's how I sold it to my mom. It was friendship. It was necessity. I made sure Viv and I were together. With a life where I'd had to work hard for everything, where I felt as if I'd raised myself, to have someone who was there when I needed her; it meant the world to me.

The world howled in pain.

I wasn't sure if I was dreaming or not. When I opened my eyes, Ryan was flailing, hopping as if he was on fire. "Get 'em off! Get 'em off!" It'd be funny anywhere else—this strong guy, screaming like a girl. He finally hopped one-legged into the water seeking escape.

By now all of us were up.

Ryan emerged, soaked, a cluster of small welts rising from his arms. Something had bitten him. Out of the water, his body was taut, his hands fists, and he let out a throat-clearing scream that echoed through the jungle.

Nico asked, "You all right, man?"

He continued to clench in agony.

"Ryan?"

He uttered one word: "....pain...."

"What happened? What bit you?" My feet dangled over the bamboo and I quickly pulled them up. I peered over the bed, but only saw dirt.

Derek said calmly, "Probably bullet ants. They hang around the base of trees. And their sting is...." He motioned to Ryan as evidence.

"Why didn't you tell me?"

"I did."

"Not that they bit! Not that they—" He clenched again, his body contorted as if being shot by an unseen laser beam. If Ryan Wray felt pain, then those bites must've been off the Scovell scale. Ryan made his way back to the base of the tree and took his revenge. He kicked and scraped his foot against every bullet ant he found. "Take that you ugly shits." He used his crutch and made paste of their bodies.

When he finally calmed down, he asked, "What else is dangerous out here?"

Derek smirked. "Pretty much everything."

That was the understatement of the year.

I had slept, but my body was thrashed. Waking crystallized what I'd feared: I was bruised and sore, as if my body had been turned inside out. Anything for an aspirin. Or dry clothes. Morning came with a new malady: hunger. My stomach rumbled. The last meal I'd had was the terrible airplane food, which I'd barely touched. My mistake. How I'd love a piece of that congealed patty they called meatloaf.

Then I realized what I was really suffering from: disappointment. I thought we'd wake up like a collective Sleeping Beauty to find a handsome rescuer next to us. But we were alone. On our own.

I looked at the blue sky and saw no planes. Not even a vapor trail. Who knew how far we were from the crash site?

I could feel the weight of despair descend on me. I didn't want to move from my bamboo bed. I didn't want to move at all. Viv scampered over to me. "Come with me." Even here, under these conditions, she seemed effervescent.

"Where?"

"I have to go…." She nodded towards the privacy of the jungle. "I didn't want to ask Nico."

Making sure to avoid any ants, we carefully made our way a few yards into the jungle.

Viv said, "You always know how to fix things. Tell me it's going to be all right."

I wanted to believe it. "It's going to be all right."

She squatted and did what she needed to do. I looked away. A mist hung in the trees, like diffused cotton balls, and for a second it looked like the beauty of a postcard. I hated that image for seducing me with its splendor, its false sense of security.

When Viv was done, she pulled up her pants and covered the spot with dirt.

"I'm not cut out for this, Em."

"None of us are."

She said, "The jungle...it's everywhere. There's no where else to look."

"Look at me." I forced a smile for her benefit. "Remember how I helped you pass Algebra II?"

Her eyebrows rose in apprehension. "You'll tutor me out of here?"

"We'll call this Survival 101. With your charm and my...I don't know, what do I have?"

"Brilliance."

"Of course. We'll be just fine."

My mini-therapy seemed to help. We walked back to the group when we heard rustling nearby. Leaves trembled a few feet from us. A black boar snuck its head from the undergrowth, short tusks at its side and it sniffed. This was no cute pig. I'd read they were carnivores and could attack if provoked.

Viv saw it and turned, ready to run. I reached out and grabbed her. "Don't move," I whispered. "Stand your ground."

Viv's eyes were huge, and for once I felt how her size must have terrified her.

"Just walk slowly backwards, okay? Don't make any jerky movements and we'll be fine. Tell me you understand."

"I understand."

The boar turned its head and looked at us.

We slowly took a step backwards. Then another.

The boar held its ground.

Once we were a few feet away, it sniffed, finding something else it was more interested in and trotted away.

Viv released her breath. "Ohmygod. I wasn't breathing."

I tried to calm her down. "I think you just passed your first pop quiz." Looking further, I saw the group was up and about. They were waiting for us.

Viv ran to Nico. "There was a boar!"

Molly rose, freaked. "A boar?"

Nico held Viv, offering comfort.

Derek said, "Boars won't attack a group. He was probably just looking for easy prey. He'll leave us alone as long as we stay together."

Ryan tried to joke. "I wouldn't mind some bacon right about now."

We congregated near the river. "Where are you going?" I asked.

Ryan said, "We gotta keep moving."

Anxiety rose within me. "We've got beds *here*."

Ryan said, "We need to find a village."

"Why? We've got a camp. We can stay…."

"Emily, it's not close enough to the crash site, and it's not close enough to a village. We're in the middle."

The middle of nowhere, I thought. The middle of hell.

Before we left, we wrote in large block letters in the mud: HELP US. We included an arrow the length of a room pointing in the direction we were heading. It looked like footprints on a sandy beach, and I wondered if anyone would ever see it.

We trudged through the overgrowth, careful to hold the branches in front of us so that they didn't snap back to hit the person behind us. My body felt as if it had mutinied against me.

Nico came up behind me. "How are you holding up?"

He made me uncomfortable. "Okay, I guess. Why aren't you up with Viv?"

"Just used the bathroom, that's all. On my way."

As he passed me, I saw the silver watch on his hand. "Does it work?"

He took it off. "Nope. Broken as all get out. But my dad gave it to me when I got straight As." He looked at me pointedly. "I like to think some things can be fixed." With that, he passed me.

The mood was dreary and after a few minutes, Nico busted out with a chant. "*I saw a birdie flying in the sky.*" He motioned for us to repeat it after him. "C'mon, people, get with the spirit."

Ryan said, "You're talking nonsense."

"No, man," Nico said. "My grandfather was in the Army. He taught me a bunch of these. Should hear some of the dirtier ones." He said it louder: "I saw a birdie flying in the sky."

I replied, weakly, "I saw a birdie flying in the sky."

Nico smiled. "Now, was that so hard? *I got some white stuff in my eye.*"

This time Viv joined in with me. "I got some white stuff in my eye."

Nico was on a roll now. "*Is that water? Is that spit?*"

We repeated, Ryan joining us. "Is that water? Is that spit?"

Nico said, "*Oh, no, it's birdie shit!*"

One by one we joined him in his marching chant: "Oh, no, it's birdie shit!"

From then it was a game of Nico chanting and us repeating: "*Oh, birdie birdie in the sky/Why did you do that in my eye?*"

Against all odds, we laughed. It was my first genuine smile and the small piece of joy reminded me of how I felt around Johannes—that sense of aliveness. I lost myself in the memory of our first kiss.

Since I'd seen him at the poetry reading, something invisible had been building between us. I'd felt a shiver of anticipation when his finger would linger ever so briefly on mine as he passed back our graded papers. How I looked forward to those moments, eternities of waiting followed by explosive Big Bangs.

He'd arranged a one-on-one with me to talk about my short story assignment. I could tell he was nervous, energy radiated from him, around me, around us. It was chemistry, that elusive quality that makes no sense unless you've felt it yourself. We were pulsing.

I could barely concentrate.

He handed me back my short story. "I think this is a real contender for *Shades of Light*." It was our school's literary magazine.

"I guess that means it's a shoo-in if you're the editor-in-chief."

"I wouldn't want you to get a big head."

He was so close. His eyes were green and flecked with shards of gold. I could lose myself in those eyes.

Surprising myself, I lunged forward and kissed him. His mouth tasted of honey and saltwater taffy. I don't know where I got the confidence to do it. It was so outside who I was. But when you know, you know.

This is how I knew he felt the same: he didn't pull away.

Not right away.

He pushed back a lifetime later, breathless, and looked at the open door. No one was there. He stepped back from me and there was fear in his eyes. "You're underage."

I felt stupid. So so stupid. What was I thinking? I tried to soften everything. "I'm seventeen." As if that made it any better.

"I'm your *teacher*." He whispered, "I could get fired."

"I won't tell anybody…I'm sorry."

I ran to the door when he reached for my arm. "Emily, wait." I turned and gazed at him.

"Are you recording this?"

"What? No." I showed him my phone. It was off.

"I didn't know if someone put you up to it. Like a joke. Or a dare."

"No. Never." This was making everything worse. He was going to make me say it. He wanted to hear me say *why* out loud. "Please, Mr. DeKoning. I'm embarrassed enough."

"There had to be a reason. Something I did…."

What could I tell him? That it was everything he did? Even though I felt rejected, I knew the truth. I wasn't crazy. This wasn't one-sided. I'd *felt* it.

"Don't you feel the same?"

He shook his head. "…I can't."

"What about all the books and poetry we read about forbidden love? How nothing can stop the human heart? Not war, not rules, not families. Think of

Romeo and Juliet. Lady Chatterley. Lancelot and Guinevere."

"And look how they turned out."

It wasn't an answer, but it was enough. We found each other's eyes. "I'm sorry," I said. "I can't say sorry enough. It'll never happen again."

I saw something in him shift, like we were back at the café. "Won't it?" He grabbed my face, kissed me, and my world ended and began anew. From that moment on, I was his.

CHAPTER FIVE

I lay in Johannes' bed, inhaling the scent of his floral laundry detergent. The journey from our first kiss to his apartment was faster than he wanted and slower than I did. I learned about the relativity of time: days or weeks were nothing to Johannes; to me they were unendurable infinities. Yet, most of the time, we would just end up cuddling. We kissed; we messed around, but we never slept together. Not like that. I think it was his way of drawing a line. He wanted to wait, and though disappointed, I was willing.

I'd had sex before—only once—but I'd never been in a relationship, and I wasn't exactly sure how to act. I was learning by experience. I'd read books, seen movies, but those relationships were fictional; I never knew anyone that acted like people did on screen, so sure of themselves, so relaxed in their own skin. Where did that leave me?

I didn't want him to think of me as a *girl*. I wanted to be a woman.

He napped next to me, his snores like a purring bunny. His apartment was small, purposely close to school to avoid a long commute, and it was lined with books, stacked Tetris-like along the shelves. He told me he liked the feel of a book in his hand, the smell of the pages, and the sense of history that people had actually touched it.

I rolled out of his bed and stood up. My toes curled into the carpet. There weren't posters of rock stars or women in bikinis on the wall—this was a man's room. Instead, there were photos. As I looked closer, they were of him in Africa, standing next to smiling young children. They appeared to be in a crudely built school. It must've been from his time in the Peace Corp. He seemed to live his life whereas I merely existed. I wanted what he had, to take his sense of purpose as if by osmosis. The only oddity in his room was a stuffed Mickey Mouse on his desk.

I heard him stir.

"How long did I sleep?"

"Not long," I said. "What's with Mickey?" I reached over and picked him up and imitated his cheery, chirpy voice. "Hi, Johannes. I'm a mouse that talks. Why am I in your room?"

"When my parents moved from Amsterdam to America they wanted to move someplace happy. Someplace sunny." He shrugged. "They picked Disneyland."

"You grew up in Disneyland?"

"Near Disneyland. Anaheim."

I placed Mickey back on the desk. "I went there once. Saw the parade. I think it was my 10th birthday." I plopped down next to him. "Maybe you can take me there. We'll wear disguises." I laughed. "I know exactly who we'd be."

"Who?"

"Hubert Humphrey and Lolita. Oh snap!"

He mimicked a gut punch. "Low blow. Low, low blow."

We fell into a comfortable silence and I wished I could stay here forever.

"Anyone ever tell you," he said, "you smell like puppy?"

"I smell like a dog?"

"*Puppy*. There's a difference. Like…mother's milk and joy. Somebody ought to bottle and sell it. They'd make a mint."

I tried to find the scent on myself, to no avail.

"I had a puppy growing up," he said. "Smelled so sweet butterflies would literally land on his head."

"I guess there's worse things to be."

"Nothing better."

"Do you think I'm pretty?"

His face crinkled. "What an odd question."

"That's not an answer."

"You're beautiful."

I hated when I heard my mother's voice in my head telling me I was average. I hated the insecurities that bubbled up within me. I wondered what it would take for them to go away. "What happens when I turn 18?"

"What do you mean?" He pulled me next to him and kissed my cheek. "I think you turn into a pumpkin. Oh, wait, that's at midnight."

"Will we be able to, you know, go out in public?"

"Only after you graduate."

That was an entire year away. A lifetime. "What if I transferred?"

"To another school?"

I nodded. "Or dropped out."

"No. No way. This is your education. One of the best around. I won't allow it. Not on my account."

He sensed something change in me and said, "What?"

"I love you." I'd never told anyone that before. But I loved this man, this gentle, smart man. I was amazed how easily it rolled off my lips. He looked confused. "You don't have to say it back. I get it. I just wanted you to know."

"I do. I most definitely do." He rested his head on my thigh. "It's complicated, that's all."

"Everything's complicated," I sighed.

When I had my period, my mother took me to an Olive Garden. We sat in a booth and she told me to order whatever I wanted. A handsome waiter probably a few years out of college gave recommendations and my mother was smitten. He took our orders and we were alone.

Our menus gone, the table felt empty. It was only she and I, sitting across from each other, Dean Martin songs playing in the background. It was unlike being at home where we passed each other, coming and going, muttering hellos and goodbyes. Actual conversation was an endangered species. Rather than feel excited at this mother-daughter bonding, I was uncomfortable. There was something forced, something fake. While I felt invisible most the time, at least it seemed natural.

"When I was your age," she said, "do you know what my mother did after I got my period?"

"Mom," I said, not wanting patrons to overhear.

"She didn't do anything. It's like she didn't know. Or didn't care. I knew if I ever had a little girl, I'd sit her down proper and celebrate her awakening."

This was the thing my mom chose to celebrate? This biological thing I had no control over? Not my French horn recital or the spelling bee I almost won. This.

My mom was always on the dramatic side, given her interest in acting. It's the reason she came out to Los Angeles in the first place. She was the belle of the ball at her Minnesota high school and once she graduated, came out west. Maybe I inherited some of her need to escape: I weaved scenarios where I was caught in a Cinderella story and my mother was just a placeholder. I would create alternate versions of my life, daydreaming.

"Do you have any questions? Anything you want to ask? The things I could tell you, believe me…."

I shook my head. I already knew the whole birds and bees spiel. She seemed disappointed that I didn't take her up on her offer to relive her glory days.

"Well, there are a few pearls of wisdom I figured I'd share. I'd like to think somebody could learn from my mistakes. At least they'd be worth something. Are you listening?"

"Yes," I sighed.

How could the person who raised me be such a stranger? I wondered if she would ever know me.

She asked, "Are you sure?"

"I'm right here." What more did she want me to do?

She leaned in as if telling me secrets of the universe. She paused, waiting dramatically for maximum effect: "Never trust anything with a penis." She sat back with a self-satisfied look. "If there's any piece of advice that's better, I haven't heard it."

I didn't know what to say. I almost asked her to repeat it so I could laugh when she said penis.

Her warning wasn't without merit. She never did find her star on the Hollywood Walk of Fame. Instead, my mother got knocked up by a musician who she never saw again. That is about as brief an explanation as I got as to my origin. (No, I'm not the daughter of a famous rock star. I am the daughter of a guy who sweet-talked my mom with a six-string and then disappeared. My own ditty of the event goes something like this: *"This is what she told me, this is what she said, your father's long gone, 'tis better to think him dead."*)

"And the other thing," she said. "You may not think it, but you have it better than me."

"What are you talking about?"

"Oh, waiter?" She smiled and he smiled back (probably for a tip), but it was like catnip to her. "Can I get a lime in my water?"

"Sure thing." He knew just how to work her. "I have to ask: are you sisters?"

Soooo lame.

But my mother ate it up. "Oh, I wish. I'm her aunt." I don't know why she lied. Maybe not to scare off potential suitors who were scared of dating moms. The waiter left.

This was supposed to be about me and like usual she made it about her.

"What was I saying? Oh, men."

"No, that I had it better."

"Right. See, being average is a blessing. You'll never have to deal with problems that beauty brings. The lies and complications from men. The jealousy and cattiness from women. You must know by now that some women are the worst. There are those in the Sisterhood and those in name only. Always be a sister, Emily. There's nothing worse."

"Not Hitler?"

"Yes, Hitler. Of course he's worse, smarty-pants. But honestly, not by much." She bowed her head, grasped the armrests of her chair and let out a few breaths.

"Mom?"

She dug through her purse, finding a small orange medicine bottle and popped a pill. "Nothing. Just felt an anxiety attack coming on."

Minutes later, our food came, noodles and sauce, meatballs and bread, lots and lots of bread. I pondered my future of being non-threatening to my girlfriends and in the perma-Friend Zone with guys. Wonderful, I thought. What a life.

As we ate, I could tell my mom settled into the calm haze I recognized that came from too many Ativan. Her eyes got glassy; her gaze, unfocused. She smiled more and acted ditzier. It wasn't unpleasant, really; just not real. Not the truth. She was a fake version of herself.

I was never sure if my mother suffered from anxiety or not. I know it's what she told me, but I think she just didn't want to seem like an addict.

She twirled her fork in her pasta, circling and circling, making slow rotations. "You know, Em, sometimes I wish I wasn't pretty." Her voice was soft and dreamy. "Beauty is like wearing a mask. People only see the mask and nothing underneath."

"Mom, are you going to eat?"

She seemed to notice her twirling for the first time. "Oh."

She might have said she wished she wasn't pretty, but I could tell she missed the way men used to look at her. My mother was beautiful once—I've seen the pictures—though life has clearly sucked the youth from her. She still holds up well, but her dark hair has slivers of grey, her face is prematurely aged (cigarettes, stress), and though she's still thin, it's not a flattering thin. Maybe it's her posture; she always carries herself like someone's about to steal her purse. Apparently, I didn't get her genetic promise. I got my unknown dad's: small breasts, stumpy legs, and a face that gets passed over.

Watching my mother, I didn't know what was worse—being beautiful and then aging out of it, or like me; never having been beautiful at all.

Sometimes I feel like I'm the embodiment of her failed dreams, the reason she works at a dog boarding facility and is nowhere near being famous. Or rich. Or any of the other reasons a person craves attention from strangers. Whatever hole she needed to fill only grew deeper as I grew older. I sensed the growing promise in my life contrasted to the dying promise of hers.

And when your mother's life is more chaotic than yours, you find you don't rebel. At least not in the traditional sense. I rebelled by not rebelling.

I grew up on my own. I took care of myself. I survived.

After a lifetime living with my mother, surviving in the jungle should've been easy.

Mosquitoes swarmed around my head. Clouds of them. Their *whirr* was relentless, an earworm with no melody. There was no relief: nowhere to run, no house to escape inside, no bug repellent, and I began flailing like Ryan had earlier. I looked like a whirling dervish.

Nico saw me—he was always looking at me—and said, "Em, what's wrong?"

"The bugs! The bugs!" I just wanted it to stop.

He caught me and put his shirt over my head so that I was nestled next to his chest. I didn't want to be next to him. I wanted to run away, but I was away from the awful bugs. With light streaming through his cotton shirt I could pretend I was in bed, hiding beneath the sheets. Around me, I heard the others slapping away mosquitoes, too.

Molly asked, "Do these things carry malaria?"

Nico shushed her and said to Viv before she could freak out, "Let's worry about that later, okay?"

Derek said, "Know what'll help?"

Ryan deadpanned, "Not being here."

"Mud. Put it on your skin. It's nature's repellant."

I would've smeared feces on my face if it stopped the biting, such was my vanity.

I emerged from under Nico's shirt, and Viv threw me a look. I couldn't tell what—concern? Jealousy? I ignored it and reached into the mud and slapped it on my face, arms, and neck. Everyone else followed. It dried, forming a barrier, and amazingly, the bugs left us alone.

This was only our second day, and the longer we walked, the more I felt we were going deeper into the jungle and further from rescue. I was still wet, my skin pruning, and I could smell my own breath, sharp and sour. I assumed Ryan knew the way. I vaguely knew moss only grew on one side of trees and I think he used their growth pattern as a guide.

My stomach rumbled, interrupting my thoughts. We were starving, to the point I could almost feel my stomach eating itself.

"I need food." I almost laughed out loud. I sounded so caveman: *me need food*. Yet, that's how my brain was starting to operate, as if I was getting dumber.

Food, food, food, food.

"Booyah!" Ryan stopped near a bush and found a scattering of yellow berries.

He started picking them off the bush, about to pop one in his mouth when Derek yelled, "Stop!" Ryan held the berry near his mouth; it looked so fresh, so enticing.

Derek said, "Don't eat any yellow or white berries."

Ryan said, "Why not?"

"They might be poisonous."

"Might be?"

Derek said, "Then be my guest."

Ryan hesitated. "You got any other ideas?"

"You're not going to like this." Derek searched the ground and found what looked like a large walnut. Then he used his "hatchet" and cut it open. I expected the shell to fall away, revealing something akin to an edible peanut. No such luck.

Inside, there were two or three holes, a few centimeters wide. Something white burrowed inside them. Derek knocked the nut against the tree—clonk, clonk, clonk—trying to force them out. Little by little, the white things slid forward. When there was enough to grab, Derek took ahold of one.

It was a grub, about the size of a small thumbnail.

My stomach turned before he even did anything.

Derek popped it into his mouth, chewed and swallowed. He let out a satisfying *ahhh*. "Tastes like chicken."

Nico said, "That is some sickness right there."

Ryan still held the berries in his hand. "You want them to eat *worms?*"

Derek said, "At least they're not poisonous."

We looked at the berries, such a tease of nature, and the grubs.

"Does it really taste like chicken?" Viv asked.

Derek picked out a couple more. "Try it." He handed Molly one. "Eat up, Molly. You're eating for two."

She took it, cringing.

When Viv hesitated eating, Ryan snatched hers. "It's protein. Protein we need." He slammed it into his mouth. He didn't even chew, just swallowed. Ryan looked at us standing around. "Well, what are you waiting for? Grab some nuts and let's eat."

We gathered and Derek chopped open nuts with his hatchet. We clonked the nuts against the ground, bringing forth the little grubs from their hiding places. I didn't know what they'd one day grow into and I didn't want to know. I took the white thing, and it wiggled in my fingers.

"I'm gonna need this," Nico said and broke off another bud from his marijuana stash. He ate it with the grub and joked as if talking about wine. "A good year, yes. A faint hint of earth with a gritty mouth-feel and an aftertaste of puke."

Viv held hers. Like trying a piece of sushi, she bit off a small piece. A mistake, as the grub leaked a viscous gravy, and she gagged. "Blech. Tastes nothing like chicken."

Don't think about it. Just do it.

I was so hungry. It burst in my mouth, earthy and sticky, my hunger rising and I yearned for more, thinking *we're becoming more like savages by the hour.*

CHAPTER SIX

I press the Nurse's button. I don't know what takes them so long. I would get up myself, but I've got an IV attached to my arm keeping me hydrated, along with antibiotics. I feel like a human petri dish.

I press and press and press.

My mother must be on a cigarette break.

The door opens and a nurse enters, probably expecting to find me writhing in pain, only to see a normal girl in bed. "What's the matter?"

I point at a window, which lets in a flood of light. From outside, I can see trees swaying in the breeze.

The nurse doesn't get it. "What?"

"The fly."

"The fly?"

I point. There is a lone fly buzzing on the window and the incessant *zzzt* taunts me to no end.

"It's just a fly," the nurse tells me.

"Can you kill it, please?"

She considers, and then walks out and I think she's ignoring me, but seconds later she returns with a stack of paper rolled into a man-made swatter. She approaches the window and with the determination of a predator, *swacks* the fly. It leaves a small smear.

"Can you shut the blinds, too?" I ask.

"But it's such a beautiful day." She sees my resolve and the blinds snap shut.

I used to love nature. Now I want to live surrounded by cement.

Give me four walls and streets and freeways for as far as I can see.

Give me traffic thick with rush hour.

Give me neighbors and their loud music and late-night parties.

I hear the patter of feet outside my door, and it soothes me for I know with certainty: I am not alone.

Valentine's Day. Sometimes I think there is nothing lonelier than being a single girl on that made up Hallmark holiday, that one day where there is no hiding if you're alone. Where the happiness of other couples is on display like a huge neon sign, reminding you that *you're not good enough. Not pretty enough. Not worthy enough.* I hated having to watch everyone else get flowers or cards. Smiles and holding hands and stolen kisses. *Ugh.*

Johannes wasn't my boyfriend, not really. I didn't know what to call him. So when I walked to my high school locker and opened it, I expected nothing. But inside, caught near the door's seam, was a red envelope. I slipped my finger gently under the flap and brought out the card. In simple type, it read: *Will you be my Valentine?* There was no signature, just the letter "J."

J for Johannes, I thought.

He risked getting caught slipping it in my locker.

He risked it for me.

I didn't think of myself as the gushy romantic type, but I found myself beaming, and this simple gesture made me feel loved. The energy in the school seemed to shift, as if the lights were brighter, the air cleaner. I looked down the hallway, taking part in the shared happiness, feeling like we were all part of a love parade.

Then I saw Molly. She was at her locker. She hesitated, as if by some wish, some miracle, there might be something inside when she opened it. There wasn't. She always put on a front as if she didn't care, protecting herself from hurt behind a wall of stone, but looking at her when she thought no one was watching told me everything. She was just a girl who wanted to be special.

I watched as she slammed her locker and walked off, and I knew what I had to do.

Near the end of the day, a note was placed on her locker.

I watched as Molly read the note and I followed her as she went to the front office. Through the glass windows, I spied as she signed for her flowers. They were a dozen white roses, a splash of winter in a vase. I'd had the florist write a note that read: *You are Special. From a Friend.* Her eyes squinted, puzzled, as she re-read the note. Then she lifted the roses and smelled them. But she didn't smile. She spoke back and forth with the confused-looking receptionist, motioning at the flowers. Then Molly walked out of the office. Empty-handed.

I took one last glance through the window. The receptionist took the flowers and placed them on her desk. I didn't understand.

In the hallway, I caught up with Molly.

"Hey," I said. "Saw you in there. Were those flowers for you?"

"Why do you care?"

"Just thought they were nice, that's all. Someone's a lucky girl."

"Nope."

That couldn't be right. I'd seen her go get them after reading a note on her locker. I made sure they were addressed to the right person. I didn't even want to count how many minimum wage hours I'd spent paying for them.

"C'mon, they were for you. I saw the note on your locker earlier."

She turned to me, mocking, "Are you stalking me?"

"Why lie?"

"Why ask if you already know?"

"No reason," I stammered. "They were beautiful."

"They were a joke, okay? Someone's idea of a joke." Molly tried to push away, but I caught up with her again.

"What if they weren't?"

She stopped. "Why? Did you send them to me?"

I hesitated.

Molly's voice made my answer easier. She asked, her voice laced with sarcasm, "Why, did you feel *sorry* for me?"

"No," I said. "I didn't send them."

The bell rang, and Molly sighed. "Great. Now I'm late for class."

I watched her walk off alone, unsure if I'd done the right thing after all.

The projector's cylindrical light streamed above me, dust motes floating within it. Charlie Chaplin in his herky-jerky manner as the Little Tramp worked on an assembly line, and the line kept getting faster and faster. He wasn't wearing his usual costume of hat, black suit, and cane. Instead, he wore overalls and a white T-shirt. The black & white film was accompanied by quirky music, sound effects, and occasional dialogue. It occurred to me my life had been a kind of pre-ordained assembly line of its own: school and summer, rinse and repeat.

I'd never seen a Chaplin movie before, only bits and pieces on TV, and never in a theater where it was being shown as part of a retrospective at the Silent Movie Theatre. Though the film was decades old, it still held up, and I liked it. It reminded me of an "I Love Lucy" episode I'd seen growing up. The theater was small and intimate, the seats comfortable and cushy, and it seemed to smell like old upholstery and secrets. I sat alone. Waiting.

As Chaplin got thrown from one mess to another, a figure in the dark appeared, along with the wafting of buttered popcorn. It was Johannes, dapper in his professorial sport-coat. He squeezed past a few moviegoers near the aisle, and into the open seat I'd saved for him. We were near the back, off to the side, and away from everyone else in an island of privacy.

"Sorry I'm late," he whispered, though he intentionally came late and separately, so that we wouldn't be seen together. The movie date had been his idea, something different than CIA-ing to his apartment, not that I minded camping out at his place. I enjoyed being his refugee.

We watched the movie and held hands. The Little Tramp had a nervous breakdown and was thrown into a hospital. Then he met an orphan girl. The cops were after her because she stole a piece of bread. To save her, the Little Tramp told the police he was the thief.

I wondered if a man would ever do that for me. Love me enough to do anything.

I asked, "Am I your girlfriend?" Johannes' face crinkled in a way I'd seen him when a student asked a ridiculous question. "Or am I…something else?"

"Like what?"

"Someone you see. On the side." When he didn't answer, I added, "I'd understand, you know."

He lifted my hand and kissed the back of it. "So mature, aren't you?"

"I'm serious."

Someone turned in the audience and gave us side-eye, an unspoken request to stop talking.

Johannes spoke quietly into my ear, his lips nearly touching my lobe, his breath warm. "You're my girlfriend." After a beat, he said, "Feel better?"

I admit I did.

That is until the movie ended, the lights came up, the spell broke, and people stood to go home. Immediately, we stopped holding hands. We rose from our seats, awkwardly seeing if we recognized anyone. He went one way down the aisle and I another. Then he melded with the stream of theater-goers and walked out the door. As was the plan, I waited a minute, loitering near the women's bathroom, and then exited. Outside, he was already in his car, a used Ford Escort, practical and egoless, pulling into traffic. As he passed in front of me, he didn't even wave.

I'd never felt so invisible.

We stopped to drink water from a hole. I got on the ground, digging in the mud, having a memory of being at the beach making sand castles. I'd always mocked the pollution in Los Angeles; the brown layer that hung over the basin, a sickly cloud of yellow air. Yet the brown water that pooled in the hole made L.A. seem like an oasis.

Everyone stood around, my head level with their knees. Derek had discarded his remaining shoe, preferring to go barefoot rather that walk lopsided.

I asked him, "Aren't you worried about stepping on something?"

"It's what indigenous people do." He wiggled his toes. "Everything seems ship-shape so far."

Ryan said, "You like this place too much."

Derek shrugged. I glanced at Ryan's prosthetic leg and thought at least he was safe if he startled a snake. No snakebite for him. His handicap was suddenly an asset.

The water continued to fill the hole. Once it was complete, I offered Molly the first drink. She sat next to me and slurped the water down.

The hole wasn't that big and she continued to drink. I didn't want to be rude to someone pregnant, but still. I held my irritation.

It was Viv who said, "Save some for the rest of us."

Molly rose from the trough, streaks of brown dribbling down her chin. "Sorry."

As we took turns drinking what little remained, Derek asked Molly, "So, does the guy know? About you being...?" He gestured as if he had a big belly.

She wiped her face and licked the beads of water from her hand. "No."

"You haven't told him yet?" Derek said more to himself. "Damn, that would suck."

"I can't."

"Why not? Don't you think he has a right to know?"

She paused and then said simply, "He's dead."

That silenced us. I thought of her not only being a teen mom, but of the child growing up without a father. I'd grown up without one and though I couldn't miss what I never had, I wondered what it would've been like to have a dad. I was jealous of 'Daddy's girls'. There was something inherently safe knowing that of all the guys in the world, there was at least one who had your best interest at heart.

Viv asked, "When?"

Molly didn't answer.

I understood. "He was on the plane, wasn't he?"

Molly hesitated and then nodded.

"Oh, God, Molly," I said. "I'm so sorry."

Viv asked, "Was he in our group? The Riverdale Academy group?"

Another nod.

Derek said, "Who was he then? Pete Conlin?"

Ryan waited for Molly to answer. If his friend was with her, clearly Ryan had no idea.

"No. Somebody else."

Nico said, "You don't have to say, Molly."

Derek interjected. "He's dead. What does it matter?"

Molly stood up, making some internal decision. "He was…." We waited for her to say. "He was my teacher." Molly found my eyes. "Mr. DeKoning."

The world stopped. My world stopped. I must have blanked out for a moment. Did I hear her right?

"That can't be," I said.

My voice got lost among our rapid-fire questions. *When did it start? Did he give you better grades? Did he love you?*

It couldn't be.

He was mine. He was mine. He was mine.

Looking at Molly, I thought, how could he be hers too?

My skin was flayed from my bones, my soul exposed, and no one could see. No one cared.

I hadn't even mourned him, so terrible was the idea of him being gone.

Fury welled in me, a fury that threatened to explode. No one knew my shame, my betrayal, my disappointment. All the pages of his poetry that I had sacrificed in order to save us, and now I would've been willing to use them for kindling, if we could only start a fire.

I sat in the mud, fading in and out of existence, never having felt more alone.

Viv turned to me. "Are you okay?"

Someone else spoke, but it came from my mouth, my voice. "Yes."

Derek's mouth hung open in a wide O. "You were bumping uglies with Mr. D? That is some *To Catch a Predator* shit."

"Stop it, Derek," I scolded.

Derek took a moment. "I guess you're right. Molly's 18. Okay, technically legal. But ethically? Don't get me wrong, if I was a teacher, I'd probably do the same thing. It'd be like shooting fish in a barrel."

"I don't really want to talk about it." Molly moved away from us and sat on a fallen tree.

My head swam. My English teacher had sat next to me on the flight under the guise of being a chaperone. Seemingly random. But the seating assignment had been orchestrated. I sat in the window seat, Johannes in the middle, and Viv took the aisle. In the darkness of the cabin and under a blanket, we held hands. With every bump, he gently squeezed, and his reassurance calmed me.

Then the plane jostled violently and he quickly jerked away.

That's the last memory I have of him.

My hand, my left hand, the one I held him with was now covered in mud, dirt crusted into my fingernails.

Looking at Molly, I couldn't picture her with him. She and I were not alike. We were not a "type." We had nothing in common. She could not have shared what we had. There was no way. It wasn't possible.

But falling from the sky wasn't possible, either.

I was learning a lot about what was possible and what wasn't.

I walked to Molly and stood above her. She seemed so weak just sitting there. I could've kicked her.

What is the jungle doing to me?

"I'm sorry," she said.

"Yeah, you *are* sorry," I wanted to say. Instead, I sat down and held her hand. "He was my favorite teacher."

Molly seemed surprised by my kindness. "Mine, too."

She didn't look like she was showing. "How far along are you?"

"About three months."

I did the math: I was with him three months ago. Sometimes he couldn't take my call. Sometimes he was "too busy." Now I knew why. Still, I needed a reason not to believe. "Are you sure it's…?"

"There was no one else."

Why had he slept with her and not me?

She was 18, I thought. That's why.

"May I?" I reached my hand out to touch her belly.

"You can't really feel anything," Molly said. "I think it's too soon."

She was right. I touched her skin, pressing against her to find some remnant of the man I loved, and felt nothing.

My mother's advice was right.

Molly could've been me. I could be the one pregnant. Something surged inside me, and I couldn't tell if it was relief or jealousy. I asked before thinking, before I realized that I didn't want to know. "How did it happen?"

"It started slow. He smiled at me in class. Told me I was smart."

It sounded all too familiar.

"At first, I thought he was just being friendly. Encouraging, you know?"

I thought of how he invited the entire class to watch his poetry reading. Was it a ploy?

Molly continued. "But then I got the feeling that it meant something else." She trailed off. "What am I going to do, Emily? What am I going to do?"

I honestly didn't know.

We sat on that soggy ass log holding hands in silence. I said, "If you need any help, any at all, just let me know. Okay?"

She nodded, and I helped her up. I called out to the group. "We're ready."

CHAPTER SEVEN

After the crash, I never saw my English teacher's body. At least, that's what I've told myself.

I've told myself a lot of things.

Walking in the jungle, I oscillated between anger and jealousy, and thought to myself: how could I hate Molly? She didn't intend to fall in love with Johannes. She didn't do it to hurt me. It just happened.

I knew what was right. But how I felt? That was something else. I'll say it: I didn't like Molly. Seeing her made the relationship I had with Johannes feel cheap. Maybe it always was.

I thought I was special.

He'd lied to me and I'd believed him. I'd given him my heart.

So much for love.

I fought the urge to cry. A sea of sadness crashed against me. I would not give in to it. I would not allow Johannes to reduce me any further.

As my mother might've said, you're not a woman until a man has stepped on your heart. Because only then do you realize how strong you really are.

I held the last remaining page from his book of poetry; the one with his signature, with his half-cursive, half-block letter writing. The one with *To Emily, my favorite student.*

I crumpled it up and it was so moist it nearly disintegrated in my hand. Good riddance, I thought and scattered the pieces like ash into the air.

My boss at Burger King asked me to cover the register while Derek went on break. I checked the time. Only an hour until closing. The dinner rush was over and time lagged. I was there with my hat and polyester uniform when a woman approached. She might've been in her early 40's and she didn't seem like the normal customer—no family in tow, no on-a-road-trip weariness, no quick-bite-after-work employee. She went to a professional salon, that was clear: French manicure, hair styled over the shoulder, and expensive clothes. She was trim and in shape, the kind of woman with time on her hands. Still, there was a kindness about her.

She looked at my nametag and greeted me with a warm smile. "Emily! So nice to meet you!"

"Um, hi. Can I get your order?"

"Sure. I'll have the…." She stopped and considered, her eyes scanning the overhead menu. "Oh, what the heck. I'll have the Number 2 combo meal."

"For here or to go?"

"To go." She opened her purse. She rifled through a wad of cash and handed me a twenty.

"Here's your receipt," and I gave her change. "It'll just be a few minutes."

She didn't move, still smiling. Then it hit her. "I'm sorry. I'm Derek's mother."

Once she said it I could see the resemblance: the longish face and ears that stuck out a little giving her an elfin quality. On her, they were adorable; on Derek, not so much.

"Derek's on break. Would you like me to get him?"

"No, that's all right. He doesn't know I'm here." She leaned in, as if telling me a secret. "He's told me so much about you."

"Oh? Really?"

"I'm glad he found a nice girl. You seem very nice, if you don't mind me saying that."

"Not at all." The conversation was making me uncomfortable. "What did he say?"

"As you can imagine, he's excited."

I stammered. "It's good to be excited."

"Maybe you'll come over for dinner sometime, and we can get to know you better. I know Derek can be shy about bringing people home."

I was too stunned to do anything other than agree. "Sure, Mrs. Wert."

"Please, call me Miranda." She held out her hand and shook mine. "I promise we don't bite." From behind me, I heard Derek. "Mom!" He rushed up next to me. "What are you doing here?"

"Just seeing how work is going." She turned to me. "Such a pleasure to meet you. See you soon." It wasn't a question; it was said as fact.

"Mom, what did you do?"

"Nothing." She winked at me. To Derek, she said, "See you at home, dear."

Derek and I watched her leave. As she disappeared out the door, I saw she hadn't taken her bag of food. I thought of running after her, but realized she hadn't come for the combo meal. Derek slunk away, totally red-faced.

I didn't know what Derek had told his mother and I didn't want to know. It was just too weird. I decided not to bring it up. No use making the situation weirder.

Our shifts finished and we walked to our cars together. Streetlights illuminated the parking lot. We smelled like french fries, our shoes were spattered with grease, and our polyester itched.

Don't say anything, Derek. Please don't say anything.

He asked, "So, what did she say?"

"Nothing," I lied.

"I have to know, Em."

"Really, she wanted to meet me…because I'm so personable, right?"

He let out a long sigh. "I could kill her sometimes. She thinks…you already know what she thinks."

"No, I don't."

"She thinks…." He scrunched his face, as if in pain. "…you're my prom date."

"What?" Was this his way of asking me out? I didn't know if it was ingenuous or totally manipulative. I was stunned. I hadn't given him any vibes that I was interested. I wasn't. I mean, it was *Derek,* the very definition of the Friend Zone. "That's sweet," I said. "But…."

"Don't give me the rejection line, all right? I didn't ask you, never did, wasn't going to, so please, don't. Just don't."

"Then why does she think that?"

"I had to tell her I was going with *someone.* Wasn't gonna tell her no one said yes." He distractedly kicked a few pebbles. "Never thought she'd actually show up. Moms, right?"

I felt bad for him. Deep down I knew he was just a guy who wanted to be loved. Didn't we all? I wondered which girls at school he'd asked and who'd told him no. "I'm sorry, Derek."

"I don't want your sorry. There's nothing to be sorry about. I'm still going to prom."

I tried to be helpful. "A lot of people go stag."

"I'll figure something out. If my mom ever visits again…can you tell her we had a good time?"

"I can't lie to your mom."

He threw up his hands. "You don't even know her."

"What's she gonna think when I don't show for pictures?"

He slouched against his car. "Who are you going with, anyway?"

I was going alone. I was going alone so I could sneak some time to see Johannes, one of the chaperones. But I couldn't tell Derek that. No one knew about me and Johannes. Not even Viv.

"A guy you don't know," I said. "From another school."

"Oh. I didn't know you were dating anyone."

"It's casual." More lies upon lies.

"Must be more than casual to bring him to prom."

I thought fast. "It's prom, not marriage."

He looked at me, trying to read my face. I wondered if it betrayed me. "Healthy way of looking at it. Look forward to meeting him." He got in his car. "Maybe he won't mind if I cut in for a dance?"

I couldn't tell if he knew I was lying or not. "See you, Derek."

As I watched him drive off, I thought of all the lies I'd already told. I may have seemed normal, but inside, I was suffocating under their weight.

"Are these grub things all over the place?" I asked Derek.

"Don't know," he said. "As we keep moving, there might be different kinds of plants. I can't be sure."

"Shouldn't we take as many of them as we can? Like 'to-go'?"

"Why?" asked Viv. "We won't need them, right?"

Nico said, "No, babe. We won't need them."

"Just in case," I said.

"We can't really keep 'em in our pockets," said Ryan. "They might get smushed. Not sure I want them near my junk, either."

"Here." I offered my cross-body bag. "We can use this." It made me feel good to think I was being useful.

Molly asked, "Wouldn't it be easier to bring the nuts?"

Derek said, "They'll take up too much room in the bag. And I want to make sure there's maggots in 'em."

Maggots. I cringed. Anything but that word.

We picked up as many nuts as we could find and then helped Derek break them open and banged them against the ground. For a time, we were in rhythm, one large drum circle, unified in purpose. Those moments were magical. Our limbs and hands moved in time, and though we weren't talking, we were *listening*, communicating with each other, marching to the same beat, a Morse Code of hope.

We must've collected 30 or more grubs. I scooped them into my hands and placed them in my bag. It was filled with creepy-crawlies and smelled like pungent compost.

I placed the bag across my shoulders. But it was Molly who said, "Why does she get to carry them?"

"It's my bag," I said.

The jungle was screeching and Molly's voice joined it. "But it's everybody's food."

"What do you think I'm gonna do? Run off with it?"

"I'm just thinking worst-case scenarios."

"Like what?" I'd been nice to her, and she was giving me attitude? "Newsflash: we're *living* a worst-case scenario."

The truth didn't faze her. "I used to play Monopoly with my cousin. He'd be the banker, and all the time he was stealing money."

I'm not the eye-rolling type, but this required an eye roll.

Nico said, "I don't think Em's gonna cheat anybody."

"As long as she walks in front of me," Molly said. She wanted to keep an eye on me.

I was going to ignore her but thought better of it. "Here. Take it." I offered her the bag. She hesitated. "Go on."

The bonds of our trust were breaking, and this was only the beginning.

CHAPTER EIGHT

I came back from my job at Burger King to find the apartment empty. No note from my mother. I smelled perfume, though, something tropical and sugary—the telltale sign she'd had a date. Her bedroom door was open and several abandoned outfits that didn't make the cut were strewn across the bed. Thankfully, my mother never brought her boyfriends back to the apartment. I don't know whom she dated, and I was lucky never to meet a single one. I never asked questions and she didn't tell. I only knew she would be back in a couple hours if the date went badly, or I'd see her in the morning if it went well. Her private life was private, and I happily reciprocated.

Walking through the hallway lined with cherubs and pottery angel—one of my mother's interests—I thought of calling Johannes, but he'd warned me he was busy grading papers. Feeling lonely, I called Viv.

"So, what'd you tell your mom?" I asked when she arrived.

"The usual." Viv's way of rebelling against her Tiger Mom was playing video games and a "study date" with me was the perfect alibi. She went by the handle "LUV2KILL" and loved trash-talking her online foes using a combo of swear words and everyday items, such as fuck-truck, dishwater-dick and nerd-turd. She was so addicted to video games she had callouses on her thumbs.

I once asked her how she felt about playing games when all the women in them were big-breasted and wore tight outfits. I kinda thought it was sexist, but she didn't mind. She told me playing games was about escape. She'd never be big-breasted and would never save the world, so it was cool to pretend.

She lugged her console under her arm. Like she'd done a million times before, she walked into my room and set up her game. Although my mom's two-bedroom apartment was a far cry from Viv's house with a pool, she never acted as if she was slumming.

My room was small—cozy as Viv would say; a bed, desk and beanbag. But what stood out was the collage of maps that acted as wallpaper. Floor to ceiling was covered with antique maps, nautical maps, Parisian subway maps, even fantasy maps from *Game of Thrones*. There were maps of the United States during the Colonial Era, maps of Los Angeles from the Thomas Guide days. It was a strange hobby, collecting them, but they reminded me there was more to life than this room. And some day, I hoped, I'd map out a place of my own.

Viv played a first-person shooter while I watched. I liked our time together like this—sitting on the carpet, sometimes playing, but without the pressure to talk. There was something trance-like to the game that emptied my head.

I thought of telling her about Derek and prom, but I didn't want the story to take on a life of its own.

After a few kills, Viv asked, "Why don't you like Nico?"

"What?" I said, surprised. "I like Nico."

"You never want to hang out with us."

"Yeah, I do."

Her eyes were focused on the screen. "Name me one time in the last month."

I couldn't. "I've been busy." Which was true: I'd been working, studying, and seeing Johannes.

"You think he smokes too much pot."

"I don't judge him. As long as you're not hurting anybody, I say live and let live."

She paused her game, and turned to me. She never paused a game. "I think I'm in love with him."

Hearing that made my stomach quiver. "I know."

"I've been holding out on him."

"Viv, it's not my business what you and Nico do. When it's right for you, it'll be right."

"But you've done it before. You didn't like it."

"I never said that."

"You never talk about it. I thought it was a bad experience."

No, it wasn't a bad experience. It was a drunken one. Worse—and I hate even thinking it—it was with Nico. I'd do anything to take it back. True, it was with Nico *before* Viv started to date him. But it was *after* I knew she had a crush on him. I'd always thought he was cute. There was something about his head of hair, perfectly coiffed into a mess that made me want to reach out and grab it. And that look behind his glasses that seemed to know what you were thinking. But when I talked to him I clammed up and had nothing interesting to say. I hated feeling boring in his presence, but I didn't want to say anything that would actually confirm it.

It's weird how one night can change everything. I was at a party at some random parent-less home. Nico was there. Viv wasn't. We played quarters and Flip Cup. As the night wore on, the room swayed and we ended up making out in a closet. From there, things quickly spun out of control.

There's nothing I can say that will make this story seem okay. I had sex with the guy my best friend liked and when it was done, I pulled up my pants and walked home. I walked several blocks, stumbling in the dark, taking side streets, the occasional headlights passing over me, and I felt like a criminal leaving the scene of a crime. Somewhere along the way I stopped and puked up a trifecta of wine coolers, a shot of Wild Turkey, and Pabst Blue Ribbon. Classy. Very classy.

The experience wasn't good. It happened too fast. It was clumsy and sad. In the moment, I think I was trying to live up to an ideal: I was fun! Adventurous!

I was none of those things.

I promised I would never speak of it again. Not to Nico. Not to Viv. Not even to myself. I would pretend it never happened. I am only thankful that no one saw us, so the story never spread.

After that, I ignored Nico and he slowly got the hint. A few weeks later when Viv told me she and Nico were dating, I didn't have the heart to tell her what had happened. I buried the lie. Days became weeks and weeks became months, and I was happy. Happy my lie was something in the past. Happy I had not ruined the one relationship that meant the most to me. I could actually believe nothing had happened. That night was like a movie I'd watched long ago and I was already starting to forget the plot.

"Earth to Emily...." Viv's voice jolted me from my thoughts.

"What were we talking about?"

"Sex. Doing the nasty. You know, regular stuff."

What I didn't expect was for Viv to fall in love. Not just love. All-encompassing *lurve*.

I said, "Every first time is bad. It's way more anticlimactic than you think."

"Do you wish you'd waited?"

Yes, yes, yes.

"I wish a lot of things, Viv."

"Like what?"

Changing the subject, I grabbed a controller. "Like I could kick your ass." I joined the game, and we shot at each other.

Viv would never know the truth. Not if I could help it.

Never, ever.

"You ever think," said Nico, "this is kind of like Jesus' forty days in the desert?"

We inched along. Ryan led while Viv and Nico brought up the rear.

When nobody said anything, Nico asked, "No one? C'mon, don't you see it?"

Unless the topic was food, water or rescue, none of us cared. We were sore, tired, covered in mud, our skin chafing and itchy along with a hundred other aliments. And moody. Definitely moody. Conversation had dwindled to nothing.

"Seriously," Nico said, "Jesus went into the desert. This isn't a desert, but as far as being remote, it's pretty close. Jesus fasted. So are we."

Derek said, "What's your point?"

"I'm trying to give us a different perspective. We can look at this like 'boo hoo poor us.' Or we can see it for what it is."

"And what's that?"

"A spiritual struggle."

"Nico," Viv said, "you're stoned."

"Quit being a haze, Viv. Just let me talk."

"Fine," she said. "Talk. Annoy everyone." She ran forward and walked next to me. "I hate when he gets like this." I reached out and held her hand.

"Like I was saying," Nico said. "This, right now, is what we're gonna look back on as the greatest adventure we ever had. This is what everything else in your life is going to compare to. This is what you're gonna tell your grandkids about. Changes your perspective, doesn't it? It's all a test. A test of our souls. And we gotta ask ourselves—are we passing?"

Derek said, "This experience is gonna be my college entrance essay, that's for sure."

"I'm talking about what's happening here." Nico indicated his heart. "What are we gonna take from this? How is this gonna shape who we become?" We ignored him and after a few more steps his tone changed, like telling a ghost story. "Out in the desert, Jesus met the Devil."

"Who's the Devil here?" asked Derek.

"I don't think we've met him yet."

Viv joked to me, "I think I'm dating him."

"I heard that."

I was tired of his prattle. Every ounce spent listening was energy I didn't have. "Are you saying," I asked, "that you want to spend forty days out here?"

Trapped in his own logic, Nico paused. "Hell no."

"Then who cares?" I said.

On a tree nearby, I saw a green iguana. It was perched less than two yards away, just lying there like a small ancient dragon, and *I didn't care*. Above me a sloth huddled in the branches. Two days ago I would've excitedly pointed at it and said, "Look! Look! How cute is that sloth? Doesn't he look like he's smiling?" Today I didn't care. Same with the monkeys that scampered on the tops of tree branches, seeming to follow us.

Nico said, "Em, what do you think?"

"I think we're walking in a living zoo. And I hate it."

"Or," he said, "maybe *we're* the zoo, and they're looking at us. Ever think of that?" True enough, the monkeys did seem curious about us.

Ryan stopped and turned. "Can you just go back to singing marching chants? That'd be a whole lot better for morale."

Nico stopped and considered, and then let out a long howl: "Ow-woooooohhh." He repeated it. "Ow-woooooohh." The monkeys skittered away and the sounds of the jungle went quiet, which was the freakiest thing of all. After a second, the soundscape returned.

"Damn, it's like I have magical powers."

Ryan said, "The hell are you doing?"

"Haven't you wanted to do that ever since you got here?" He let out a yodel version of the Tarzan yell, banging on his chest. When he finished, he went right into imitating a chimpanzee, scratching himself under his armpits: "who-who-who-ha-ha-ha."

I wondered if Nico was losing it.

I'd never seen Ryan move so fast on his crutch and prosthetic leg. He pushed Nico to the ground. "What if they hear you?" He gestured to the monkeys, now gone. "We're surrounded by things we can't even *see*, you get that? You have any idea what else is out there? I'm not gonna be somebody's prey."

Nico looked up from the ground and laughed. He even made a snow angel, legs and arms windshield-wiping back and forth in the mud.

Ryan said, "It's not funny."

"It's hilarious! I can communicate with animals! Who knew?"

Ryan took the end of his "crutch" and jabbed it into Nico's stomach. "Don't laugh at me."

But Nico wouldn't or couldn't stop. He tried and then burst out, convulsing at a joke only he thought was funny. "I can't help it." Nico cackled. "By the power of Grayskull, I command the apes to carry us piggy-back to the nearest tribe!"

Ryan jabbed Nico in the stomach. "Don't laugh at me!"

"You're failing the test," Nico laugh-yelled—

Something that started as a joke escalated into something dangerous. We were under tremendous pressure from all that had happened and it would find release one way or another. "Don't laugh at me!" The hits grew harder and harder, and Nico's laughs morphed into howls of pain.

"Stop it!" Viv screamed. She ran towards Ryan. "You're hurting him!"

Ryan stopped, taken aback by his own loss of control. For all Ryan's tough exterior, he wouldn't be mocked. Not for being weak. Not for having lost his legs. Not, I thought most of all, for being scared. He walked away with a look of disgust, but whether it was directed at himself or Nico I didn't know.

Viv comforted Nico on the ground. "Are you okay?"

Nico lay curled on the jungle floor, his hands over his stomach, rocking gently. He looked at us accusingly and whispered, "The spiritual test? You failed…you all failed…."

CHAPTER NINE

Viv walked with Nico. His good humor had literally been beaten out of him. As he ate another bit of bud, Viv placed her hand over his in a gesture of "please don't." He shook her hand off. Ahead of them, Ryan trudged through the jungle. He muttered under his breath, trying to rally himself: "You can do it. You can do it."

He stopped and cupped his hands to his mouth, screaming: "Hello? Can anyone hear us?" He was met with silence.

Molly asked, "What about predators now, Ryan?"

He ignored her and said, "Everyone, scream 'hello' as loud as you can."

We joined into a loud chorus of "HELLO?" Our voices echoed until we were out of breath.

Again, nothing.

Then a voice in the distance. A shrill "Hola!" from within the jungle.

"Did you hear that?" Ryan said.

I couldn't believe it. Someone else was out there. All of us perked up at the possibility of another survivor or maybe, just maybe, a villager.

Ryan motioned for us to scream again, and we did. "Hello?"

A second later, the voice replied, "Hola!" It was no auditory hallucination!

Ryan cracked the first smile since the crash. He directed us, "One more time." When the voice replied back, Ryan shut his eyes, concentrating on the voice's location. "There," he said, and took off towards it. We followed, the fastest we'd traveled, damn the branches scratching us.

Ryan kept yelling "Hello," zeroing in on the voice, awaiting the reply. We were breathless.

We were getting closer.

Almost there.

Ryan called out, "Hello?"

Then we experienced the strangest thing: the voice seemed to have moved. Teleported. We were right upon it. I could swear it. But it was no longer here.

"What happened?" Viv asked.

As we stood, Molly came up from the rear—we'd hadn't noticed that she had lagged so far behind.

Ryan said to us: "You heard it, right? We all heard it." Seeing us nod, he said, "Where'd he go?"

I screamed, my voice hoarse: "Hello? Can you hear us?"

The voice came back, I couldn't tell its gender: "Hola!"

"That way," said Derek, and we headed off for it once more, this time in a totally different direction.

Like playing "Marco Polo," we shouted, then waited for a reply, moving towards the person. I yelled, "Are you all right?" But the only response I got was "Hola!" I shouted, "What's your name?" The answer was "Hola!"

We zigzagged past trees and scrub and overgrowth. All the while, I was growing irritated at this faceless person. "Why don't you walk towards us?" No response. Was a villager playing a joke on us?

Finally, the voice was close. Just another few yards.

We turned past a tree and into a small clearing and stood dumbfounded.

There was nothing. Only green, green and more goddamn green. We looked at each other, confused. Derek saw it first. A bird. No regular bird, a macaw. A big blue parrot nearly three feet long with a splash of yellow near its head, maybe someone's escaped pet. A sound came from its beak: "Hola!"

"A bird. A damn bird."

Our hearts sank.

Ryan picked up a stick and threw it at the macaw, sending it flying away, a great burst of color in the sky.

The lushness of the rainforest seemed to swallow us. We didn't belong. We weren't welcome, and I wondered what had ever made me want to come on this trip in the first place.

I had signed up for extra shifts at work—late nights and weekends. There was a trip offered at school, and I intended to go. How many times in my life would I get the chance to visit a real rainforest and see the "lungs of the earth" before they were lost to industrialization? To see dappled sunlight on emerald leaves, crashing waterfalls and the magnificent unknown? I thought of how romantic it would be to sneak time with Johannes. We could cuddle under a constellation of stars while listening to rainfall on a tin roof.

All I needed was money, permission from my mother, and a passport. I saw my mom in the morning as she straightened her hair in the bathroom.

"Mom, can you sign this?"

I placed the permission form on the sink, along with a pen.

"What's this?"

"The school trip I told you about."

"Can it wait?"

"It's due today."

She picked up the form and held the pen over the dotted line. The tip of the pen even left an indentation, and then she stopped. "Wait a second. I thought you said you were visiting the south."

"I am."

"I thought you meant 'the south.' As in the United States. Not *South America*."

"I never said that."

"That's what I heard."

I'd brought up the trip a few days earlier while she was under the influence, knowing she would say yes. I saw that the plan had backfired. I should've given her the permission slip when she was out of it. "You weren't paying attention."

"I don't know…that's so far away."

"It's a *plane* ride."

"Can you even drink the water?"

I wanted to face-palm myself. "Mom, it's a school-sanctioned event. It'll look great on my transcript. And you don't have to pay a cent." I saw her waver. "Please. It's a great opportunity. A once-in-a-lifetime opportunity."

"Emily, there'll be other trips."

"Not like this one."

She finished curling her hair and set it down. "Careful. It's hot." She turned to me and tried to primp my hair. "I don't like the idea of you being…."

"What?" I moved back a step.

"There." She handed the form back to me. "I'm sorry, I can't let you go to South America."

"Mom, it's not, like, Iraq." She didn't budge. "Why not?"

"Because it's Paraguay."

"You make it sound like a Third World country."

"Well, it is."

"No, it's not."

"Compared to America, it is."

"Mom, they have running water, electricity, *government*—"

"Emily. The answer is no."

I saw the look she got when stubbornness overtook rational thought. "Mom—"

"And that, too. Because I'm your mother. At least for another year. Then you can do whatever you want."

I could've argued. I could've stomped and moaned. I could've said so many mean things.

But I didn't.

I took the permission slip and drove to school. I burned with anger. Then I did something that would change my life forever: I forged my mother's name and handed it in.

CHAPTER TEN

The sun was setting and I wanted to cry. I couldn't bear another night in the dark, another night in the damp, another night in the drizzle and fear. The trees seemed to form a prison of intertwining wood around us.

Viv turned to Derek. "What do we do?"

"What are you looking at me for? Ryan wanted to come this way, and you all followed along. Ask him."

The group turned to Ryan. Viv said, "How long to a village?"

Ryan threw up his hands. "How should I know? Ten feet? A mile? Hell, maybe we passed one already because I can't see shit. Can you?"

"But you said we'd find a village. You said it, and I believed you. We believed you."

"And we will! There's gotta be one along the river somewhere."

Viv looked up at the canopy that nearly blotted out the sky. "What if they never find us?"

Ryan flared. "I'm trying to stay positive here. I'm trying to stay sane. Can you help me with that? Can you just for a second, stop being such a whiny bitch and maybe do something useful?"

Nico shook his head. "Not cool, man. Not cool."

Derek rose, confusion on his face, and asked Ryan, "Why are you such a dick?"

"What?" It was clear no one ever spoke to him like that.

Derek reiterated. "You heard me. Serious question."

I don't know why Ryan didn't go after Derek. If this were school, things would've been much different. Out here, Ryan had no spectators, no reputation to protect. Or maybe Ryan was too tired like the rest of us. He leaned against his crutch and bent over, like a runner after a marathon. He seemed to mull the question in his mind. He stayed looking at the ground, as if finding an answer there.

"This one time I go swimming. Swimming like I've always done. The water seems clean enough. Few hours later, though, I'm not feeling so well. Got this headache that just *crushe*s me. Thought it was the flu. I was cold and shivering, and I had this weird rash, red splotches up and down my body. I pass out and the next thing, I'm in the hospital."

"I look down and…my legs are gone. I thought, 'That's not right,' and I went back to sleep. I must've been dreaming. Had to have been dreaming. I wake up and look again. I'm not getting it 'cause the weirdest thing is I can feel 'em. I can feel my legs right there. I can feel myself wiggling my toes. What I'm seeing and what I'm feeling doesn't add up."

"Then they told me. And you get the strangest ideas. Like, this has got to be the best prank ever. Or maybe they'll grow back. Like a tail on a lizard. You know it's not true, it's crazy, but you wish. You wish so hard. 'Cause your life is over. The life you knew is just *done*."

"They told me I almost died. At the time, I wished I had. I wasn't gonna be this…thing. I had dreams, you know? I was gonna play football. I was gonna walk. Who thinks they're gonna wake up and not be able to walk again?"

Ryan straightened up and looked at us. "With everyone crying around me, I had to be the one that didn't. Everyone around me was sad and weak-ass sorry-sacks, so I had to be strong. I spent most of that year getting homeschooled and recovering. I learned to walk again. I wore prosthetics. Every day that year I looked at myself and said, 'Ryan, are you gonna be a whiny little bitch? Or are you gonna be a man?'"

We stood around quietly taking in the enormity of his struggle.

Derek nodded. "I'm giving you a big dose of respect for that. Really. Losing my legs would put a definite damper on things. But it doesn't explain why you were a dick *before* you lost your legs. You've been an asshole since, what? First grade?"

Ryan clenched his walking stick. "What do you want from me, Wart? Do you want me to say I'm sorry? 'I'm sorry.' How's that? Will that do it for you?"

Derek thrust his hatchet into a vine. "It's so easy for you. You think you can say you're sorry and it erases everything you did? Well, it doesn't."

"What do you want, Wart?"

"I want you to suffer like I have."

"You don't know the first thing about suffering. And you should thank your lucky stars you never will. Everything you're complaining about? You bring it on yourself."

"No one *asks* to be picked on."

Ryan let out a laugh. "Really? You tried to get a porn star to come to prom. Bet your parents are real proud. And whenever you apply to college? All they need to do is Google your name and there it is. Your tweets begging Luscious Funbags or whatever her name is to come. Your creepy YouTube invites. The internet's forever, or I guess no one told you that."

Derek's face contorted as if he was having an aneurism. "For the last time, the name is Wert, not Wart."

"I'm tired," Ryan said. "I really am. I may not look it, but I am wrecked. You want to hash this out when we get back, be my guest. But for now, I'm done." He turned his back on Derek, going nowhere, just wanting a different view than of his face.

I was about to speak to break the tension, but Viv beat me to it. "We should make a shelter."

Derek turned on her. "Make your own damn shelter! All of you. You know how." Derek stomped off and hacked down some bamboo. When he finished making his bed, he tossed his hatchet on the ground and promptly lay down.

He watched us, passively, as I picked up the hatchet and did my best. I never felt so reduced to survival mode as I did holding that piece of metal wreckage in my hand. It took us twice as long to make a bed half as big. Viv slept next to Nico. I shared a bunk with Molly. As darkness fell, Ryan built a bed for himself, and under a blanket of bats and moths, we slept.

Derek's videos had gone viral, at least within the hallways of Riverdale Academy. I slammed my locker shut when I saw the double-doors open and Derek walk through. It was the exact opposite of a strut and more the walk of the condemned. Ryan stood near a group of his friends and he began to chant: "Wart! Wart! Wart!" The chant spread like a shockwave encompassing the hallway and soon everyone joined in, the metal lockers amplifying the noise.

If Derek had thought asking a porn star to prom was funny or clever, he was sadly mistaken. A clique of girls laughed, a cackle of hyenas as Derek walked past. His face was stone; the hallway, pandemonium. A teacher poked her head from out of a classroom, and seeing the cause of the commotion, retreated back inside.

Derek got to his locker and opened it, unleashing a cascade of photos on the floor. It was like a whirlwind of free money, hands reaching out, grabbing, sharing, pointing. He was prey, blood was in the water, and the students circled for the kill. The laughing increased to a fever pitch.

A photo drifted over. Someone had Photo-shopped pictures of Derek having sex with the porn star, (clearly cutting and pasting Derek's head on someone else's body). It was horribly cartoonish, horribly humiliating.

I walked over and helped him collect the photos, the chant growing in the background: "Wart! Wart! Wart!"

He motioned me away, fighting tears, struggling to keep himself together. "Leave me alone, Emily."

I helped anyway, and handed him a stack. "Don't let them get to you."

"They're not."

But clearly, they were.

Maybe it was pity. Maybe it was to take a stand against the awful tide of cruelty, but that's when I made my decision. I would go to prom with Derek Wert.

I woke in the middle of the night. Molly was snoring next to me—loud rumbles, and I was amazed she didn't wake herself up. She'd moved over in the night and had taken up most of the bed, leaving me with a sliver of bamboo, and I found myself at risk of falling off. I nudged her, but she didn't budge. I wondered what Johannes would've thought about seeing his two girlfriends sharing a bed.

Around me, the jungle was alive with sound, as if every damned bug, frog or snake was trying to outdo the other. Above me fireflies danced, lighting up like a blinking Christmas tree. There were thousands of them, an entire solar system, and I lost myself trying to count. I had the odd sense of the supernatural and half expected them to form the outline of a person and talk to me like a ghostly Obi-Wan Kenobi. "The way home is there," the fireflies-as-a-person would say and point. I would say *Thank you, I'm sorry for hating the jungle. The jungle is my friend.* The flies would disperse, the sun would shine, warming my face and clothes, and all would end happily ever after.

Of course, the flies did no such thing.

As entranced as I was by their numbers and hypnotic blinking, I became aware that fireflies weren't flies at all, but beetles. When I thought of thousands of *beetles* flying so close secreting some chemical that made them light up, their magical hold gave way.

I was about to go back asleep when I noticed a figure in the darkness. The figure stood above Ryan. I almost shouted but I recognized from his slouch it was Derek. His face was hidden in the dark. I hadn't heard him. The sound of the jungle must've camouflaged his footsteps.

I saw the glint of the moon near his side and realized it was from his hatchet.

He didn't do anything. He just stood looking down on Ryan's sleeping body, Ryan's chest a metronome, rising and falling, rising and falling.

I was paralyzed. *What should I do? What could I do?*

Seconds passed and Derek did nothing, the hatchet rubbing lightly against his thigh. He turned towards the rest of us, as if to see if there were witnesses. I shut my eyes.

Moments later, I heard him step back to his bed.
I peeked: Ryan was still breathing. Still alive.
I'm not sure I slept the rest of the night.

CHAPTER ELEVEN

I'm waiting to find my purpose. I've read about people who survived cancer and found a new lease on life. That hasn't happened to me yet. I survived what my counselor calls a "tragic event." Then why don't I feel more relief? Why don't I want to travel the world, follow some obscure passion that would make me whole, or learn to play guitar? The counselor calls it depression and to give it time.

I call it fear.

I feel like those kids who cheated Death in all those Final Destination movies where one by one, Death came back to claim what was rightfully his. Or that I'll wake up and find that being in the hospital has all just been in my head—that these are my final thoughts—and I'll find myself back on the plane taking my dying breath.

I pinch myself to make sure it's not true.

I know it's not true.

I am here, in this hospital, with a second chance.

I have no idea what to do with it.

I wonder if I deserve it.

Streams of light filtered through trees and here was the dappled sunlight I'd yearned for. I stretched and sat on the bed, contemplating whether to say anything to Ryan. The tension from the previous night seemed gone, and to bring up Derek's *oddness* would only invite trouble. In fact, Derek wasn't around. His bed was empty. In the mud, a trail of footsteps led into the jungle. I scanned nearby trees—not that I could see very far—but he wasn't there. I waited a minute or two in case he was squatting somewhere. He didn't appear.

"Anybody see Derek?" I asked.

The others leaned up on their makeshift beds. Their hair disheveled, their clothes filthy, they looked like feral children raised by wolves.

Nico said, "He's probably taking a leak."

I called out. "Derek?" No response. "Derek!" I looked back at the group. "You don't think he would've run off, do you?"

Nico said, "Where's there to go? He'll show up."

Then I wondered: did Ryan do something to him?

There was movement in the woods, and just like that, Derek emerged holding a bunch of mushrooms, so many they seemed ready to topple from his crossed arms.

Nico said, "What'd I tell you?"

I chided myself for being paranoid and asked, "Where'd you go?"

"Foraging." Derek seemed in his element, more so than his weary existence at school. Here he was relaxed; here he was in control. Derek sat down on his bunk and laid out his bounty. Some of the mushrooms looked like puffy golf balls, others like umbrellas, and some were tinged yellow and looked like dried, wilted flowers. "Breakfast."

We looked over with jealousy, unsure if it was his breakfast or ours. My stomach gurgled. Viv said, "Is that an invitation?"

"Of course. Mi casa, su casa." Derek waved us all over. "That includes you, too, Ryan."

Ryan grunted from his bed, "I'm fine."

"Here." Derek tossed a mushroom and by sports instinct Ryan caught it. "There's more where that came from."

Too hungry to ignore the gift, Ryan bit into it and then gobbled the whole thing down, cap and stem.

Derek said, "Look, I want to say something. I was out of line last night.

Like Ryan said, we're all tired. I'm tired. Sorry I took it out on you all. You, too, Ryan." Derek reached out his hand. "We cool?"

Ryan took a moment, made a decision and grabbed his crutch and walked over. Then he shook Derek's hand. "We're cool."

Derek played host and passed out the assorted mushrooms. Viv and I got the yellow ones. Molly, Nico, and Derek took the golf-bally ones. Ryan got the umbrella ones. We ate and chewed and in comparison to the grubs, it was nice to have something with texture, even if they shared the same mealy taste.

Ryan said, "You really learned all this from the Boy Scouts?"

Derek nodded. "A lot of it. Merit badges and stuff. That, and my dad owns a camping supply store chain."

Ryan spoke with his mouth full. "I've been camping, but it was never camping-camping. More like car-camping. Where if you need something, you just open the trunk or ride out to the nearest convenience store. Guess that doesn't really count."

Derek said, "It counts."

Viv said, "I'm not much of a camper. As you can probably tell."

I said, "I think we've all had our share of the Great Outdoors." We enjoyed the silence of eating, bonding as if at a dinner table and the world was our dining room.

Viv asked, "Should we turn back around?"

Derek caught Ryan's eye and answered. "We've come this far. It's best if we keep going. Besides, Emily left a trail. They'll find it. And then they'll find us."

I rinsed my face in a puddle, trying to keep a semblance of routine, a semblance of normality, and caught my face in the reflection. I was happy to recognize myself. My face was scratched, dirty of course, my eyes sunken, and I seemed older somehow. My hair was a rat's nest, but nothing a good shower and a ton of conditioner wouldn't fix. The reflection reminded me I was human and healthy. I would take good news where I could find it.

We started off in our usual line, and after about an hour's walk, Ryan suddenly stopped. His face took on the appearance of someone who was about to puke. He hopped out of sight, behind some scrub. We heard his gastrointestinal distress, cringing at the violent sound.

Ryan reappeared, his face slightly pale. He waited a moment, then grabbed his crutch and moved on. We weren't worried, we'd been eating grubs, mushrooms, and basically drinking watered-down mud, after all. Until he stopped to do it again.

No one asked him anything. He was clearly not okay, but there was nothing we could do. We all had a multitude of irritations, whether it was a rash in our nether regions, sore feet, or too many bruises to count. There was nothing to be done but bear it and keep moving.

To keep his spirits up, I asked him, "What are you gonna study in college?"

Ryan rose from the bushes looking whitish-gray. "Sports medicine. Or speech. Like that guy who inspires people? You know who I'm talking about. The tall guy with big teeth?"

"Tony Robbins?"

"Yeah, him. Motivational guy."

"I think you'd be good at it."

"Nah, I'd probably just yell like my dad does." He put more effort into walking and more weight onto his crutch.

"Some people like that approach. Drill sergeant-style." I walked with him, holding branches away from his face, and he seemed to appreciate it.

"So hot out here." Big beads of sweat formed on his forehead and he wiped them away. "What about you, Em? What are you gonna major in?"

"I haven't even thought about it. I still have to graduate."

He was breathing heavily. "Must've crossed your mind…."

"I don't know. Maybe writing?"

"Writing? No one makes a living writing."

I guess growing up without a lot of money made me less focused on it. "Have you studied the ancient poets?" I saw his look and said, "Never mind."

He paused and held up his hand, looking queasy. A second later he said, "False alarm." He motioned for me to continue. "Go on. I need to concentrate on something other than…this."

"The ancient poets used to write about war. Battlefield deeds. Who was worthy and who wasn't. Who deserved to live on, if only in stories. They made people immortal, really."

"You should major in history."

"You don't get it. The writers *wrote* the history. They decided what to tell."

Ryan paused again, this time longer. I said, "Why don't we stop?"

"No stopping." He was growing weaker by the step. "Gotta treat myself the way I'd treat everybody else." He clomped through the jungle, but he was slowing down, slower than the rest of us, and Nico, Viv, and Derek passed him. So slow, in fact, that even Molly passed him, and Ryan and I brought up the rear.

As I helped Ryan navigate over bushes and beneath branches, he said, "Why are you being so nice to me?"

"Why not?"

"I was never nice to you."

"You were never mean, either." This seemed to define pretty much all of high school.

"That's not saying much." He nearly tripped and I felt his weight fall onto my shoulder. He almost knocked me over. I steadied myself and steadied him. "Can I tell you a secret?" He whispered, "I'm scared."

Ryan Wray couldn't be scared. If he was scared, what did it mean for the rest of us? Fear was contagious, and I didn't want to get infected.

"We're all scared."

"The way I'm feeling…it reminds me of before…." He stopped and rubbed the stump of his leg. "I can't do it again. I can't wake up with no arms."

"It's probably food poisoning. It'll pass." I thought of what he'd said to Molly. "You can do incredible things if you put your mind to it. You can. You will."

"I will." He silently repeated it over and over as we inched along. Suddenly, he lost purchase on his stick and toppled to the ground.

I tried to help him. He lay on the ground, not moving, releasing sad moans. "Ryan, get up." He tried to come onto his knees and fell back down. "Get up," I said. Trying to get through to him, I said, "Don't be a whiny bitch. Get. Up."

"I…can't."

I called out to the group ahead. "Hey! Wait up! It's Ryan!"

As they turned and walked back, they seemed surprised Ryan was on the ground. I said, "He's sick. Really sick."

Nico squatted next to Ryan. "He's not going anywhere. Not on his own."

Derek said, "I don't know…we can't stop."

I said, "What are you saying?"

"I'm just being practical. We can barely move ourselves."

Viv turned to Derek. "You wouldn't leave me, would you?"

Derek said, "We have to save ourselves. We save ourselves, we save him. We'll come back."

"For all the ants and snakes and whatever else is out here?" I said. "He wouldn't last a night." There had to be a solution. "I'll carry him." When they looked at me as if I was crazy, I said, "You made beds out of bamboo. Can you help me make something to drag him on? Like a stretcher?"

It took some time, but with all of us helping, we made a stretcher out of bamboo and rolled Ryan onto it. I lifted the front, carrying the bamboo poles on my shoulders, and Ryan lay sloped on the stretcher. As I held the poles, he began to slide off.

"This isn't going to work," I said. "I'm gonna need help."

No one volunteered. Out of us, Nico looked the strongest. "Nico?" He hesitated and I added, "We'll rotate. No one will have to carry him the whole time." With that, Nico stepped behind me and lifted the poles.

"Sorry, Ryan," I said. "But this is gonna be a bumpy ride."

CHAPTER TWELVE

Carrying Ryan was an ordeal. Sweat dripped into my eyes, stinging, and I couldn't wipe it away. Even with his missing leg, he felt as if he weighed 200 pounds. It couldn't have been comfortable for him, either. Nico and I swayed, and Ryan jerked back and forth in an off-kilter rhythm.

My arms gave way and I dropped the bamboo poles. Ryan crashed into the muck. "I'm sorry, I'm sorry." I tried to pick up the bamboo, but I had no more strength. My arms were noodles, loose and numb. Nico gently laid down his end. Ryan lay on the stretcher, eyes shut, as if mentally transporting somewhere else.

I said, "Viv, can you switch with me?"

"I can try." She walked to my side and took the poles in her hands. She seemed as thin as the bamboo.

I instructed, "Lift from your thighs, not your back."

She strained, trying to lift. "He's too heavy, Em." Viv looked to Molly. "Can you try?"

Molly hesitated as if she'd waited for this moment her whole life. "What'd he ever do for me?"

"Does it matter?" I asked.

"Did he ever help me when his friends called me a genetic malfunction? No. He laughed." She looked down at him. "Not so funny now, is it? C'mon,

Ryan, let's hear you laugh." When he didn't respond she walked over and nudged him with her foot. "Why isn't it funny? You laughed before. Let's hear you laugh." He still didn't make a sound. "Coward."

She glanced over her arms and put her hands around her wide waist. "Not a bad day to be fat, is it? You'll all starve to death, but I'll keep walking." She looked us over one by one, mud on our faces, hair askew, hunched over and tired. "How you feel right now is how you make me feel everyday."

"He's going to die," I said. "Is that what you want? Would that makes things equal in your book?"

"I wonder if you'd all try and carry me."

"Molly, we're dealing with what's happening right now."

Molly considered and peered down at Ryan. "If I do this, you will be in my debt, understand? Say it."

Ryan mouthed, "I understand."

"You will apologize to me."

His lips were white and cracked. "I apologize."

"Ooohh, it's not that easy. You'll apologize to me in front of your friends. Your hilarious friends."

He nodded.

"And then you will take me out to the most expensive, exclusive dinner you can afford followed by a concert with front-row seats at the Hollywood Bowl and you will post pics of us all over Instagram saying you had the greatest night ever. Do you understand?"

"I understand."

She wiped her hands. "Then let's get this show on the road." She reached down to the poles, grunted and lifted the stretcher. "You better remember this, Ryan Wray. This genetic malfunction helped save your life."

It wasn't called a rainforest for nothing. It drizzled nonstop. Sometimes it rained. Sometimes it turned into a downpour for minutes at a time and just as inexplicably as it started, it would stop. The first time it happened was curious, the idea of being caught in the rain, our sins being washed away. By the second or third, we were over it and simply hated being wet. By the fourth and fifth, we felt mold growing in our damp clothes.

This time the rain didn't stop. It came down in sheets, the undergrowth beneath us already soft to begin with was getting sticky, sucking our shoes into the muck. Any fantasies I ever had of running naked in the rain disappeared. This was misery.

The wind kicked up and the thick leaves waved, silent green applause everywhere. The sky went unnaturally dark. A storm wasn't coming; it was here, and we were caught in it with nowhere to go.

Make it stop. I'll do anything, but please make it stop.

Molly and Nico carried Ryan, but Nico slipped, flailing backwards. The shift was too much for Molly and she lost her grip. Ryan landed with a thud, crooked on the ground.

Molly said, "Everyone's gonna have to take a side."

I shook my head. My arms were still wasted.

Derek and Viv shared the front while Molly and Nico took the back. They lifted Ryan, and I walked ahead of them, holding back branches. The rain poured, mocking our efforts. They walked less than a minute before Viv's foot got caught and they came to a stop.

Nico yelled something, his mouth an angry O, but it was lost in the wind.

Viv screamed back, "Stop moving! I'm stuck!"

"Everybody take a step back," I said. They did, and Viv wrangled her foot from beneath some tree roots. Holding onto Ryan's stretcher, they moved stutter-step, like movers moving a heavy couch through a small door.

The rain pelted us, each drop a tiny bullet.

The mud was turning into a sloshy soup. More yelling from Viv. "I can't! I can't!" As she set down her end, the others screamed for her to hang on. Once Viv let go, they all released their grip, and Ryan lay on the stretcher.

We squatted on the ground, seeking shelter, our bodies bent, backs rounded. It poured and poured and I wouldn't have been surprised if it poured blood. That's how I felt about this evil place.

Molly was crying, her tears melding with the rain.

Viv and Nico looked like wet, forlorn dogs. Only Derek, the survivalist among us, seemed to enjoy himself, his face lifted to the rain.

In an effort to raise their spirits, I made a call back to Nico. "Remember! It's an adventure! It's only an adventure!" No one bothered to respond.

Rain fell and rivulets of water streamed over the stretcher. The mud was turning into a small stream.

Derek said, "Guys, we gotta go."

We looked at him, set like statues. In the storm, no place seemed better than any other.

"This is low ground. We're in danger of a flash flood." The evidence was under our feet. The rivulet was growing stronger with each passing second.

Ryan spoke, his voice weak, and I leaned in to hear him. "Don't leave me."

"We won't."

But Derek was already on his feet, walking away from the stretcher towards higher ground.

"Derek," I called out. "We need your help."

He turned his head, still walking. "I'm tapped out."

"Come back here!" I looked at the others. No one made a move.

Nico sighed, exhausted. "I've been carrying him the whole time."

"It'll only be a few more yards." It was a lie: but it sounded better than the truth. "Screw the stretcher, let's just get out of here." I got up and grabbed Ryan's arms, wrapping my hands around his. My action inspired the others to follow. Nico grabbed his prosthetic leg. Viv and Molly placed their hands under his stump, as if carrying a tray. The four of us walked octopus-style and I couldn't see but a foot in front of my face, my eyes small slits against the rain.

I felt the water rise to the top of my tennis shoes. Seconds later, it was near the top of my ankles. My mind drifted to the things in the water—snakes, leeches, worms, parasites—and I forced myself to think of better things. I grasped at happy memories.

Did I even have happy memories?

I thought of long-forgotten images: going horseback riding above Beachwood Canyon, trotting along on a horse, amazed at the gentle and beautiful power of the creature beneath me; walking into the ocean for the first time as a wave crashed over me, and I went tumbling, sand caught in my bathing suit; reading to my mother, switching roles at my request, and me tucking her in, rolling the covers up to her chin. My mother had brought me to all those places for birthdays or getaways, and there was love there. Small bits of love that kept me fed until the next time, and I knew that I wasn't alone and never had been.

The water was nearing my knee. The current pushed against me.

We sloshed and waded, and we carried Ryan like a fallen soldier. Every second was torture. Ryan slipped from my grasp. I dug into his hand, my fingernails into his skin, and I heard him yelp, but it was the only way I knew to keep ahold. My thighs burned, my back threatened to give way, but we kept moving, our distance measured by sticks; just one more tree, then another. We followed Derek up the incline, and the water lessened, receding from knee to calf, from ankle to the bottom of our shoes, and finally, mud—wet, wet, mud.

We stopped near a tree, gasping for air and sat down. Where we'd walked from didn't exist anymore: the ground had become a torrent, leaves and god knew what else floating on the surface.

We'd done a good thing. We'd saved a person. We'd chosen sacrifice over selfishness.

It was to be our last time.

CHAPTER THIRTEEN

I worked the drive-thru window. It was night, and while most people were pleasant, every once in a while I'd get a group of hemmers-and-hawers who couldn't decide on what to order. *There are only so many choices, people!* Then there were the drive-thru squatters who slowly checked their order while holding up the rest of the line. One guy, he wasn't even old (I have more patience for the elderly) paid for his meal in pennies. Pennies! The saddest ones were those who came every day by themselves, drowning in food, as though they wore a sign that read "Life Hates Me." I was extra nice to them, realizing our interaction might be the highlight of their day. Otherwise, I empathized with anyone who worked with the general public because I had proof-positive most of them were idiots.

Over the intercom, a guy ordered a burger, fries, and shake. He paid in the first window and then rolled up to get his food. I recognized the car. It was Nico's, a green Prius, another gift from his parents for maintaining a high GPA. I thought Viv might be in the car with him, but the solo order told me he was alone before he even pulled up.

I didn't want to see him. I looked for someone to take my place at the window, but the other employees were busy at their stations.

Stuck where I was, I said, "Hi, Nico," and handed him his food.

He turned down his radio, grabbed the bag and placed it on the empty passenger seat. Unfortunately, no other car was behind him so he had time to linger. "How's it going?"

"It's going."

"When do you get off?"

I'd learned to avoid this question, usually from late-night guys trying to be funny, due to its double entendre. "My shift is over at eleven."

He glanced at his clock dash. "It's ten-thirty now. How 'bout I wait and we can hang out?" He jiggled a plastic baggie filled with green and said in a singsong voice, "Got something that might make you hap-py."

I motioned for him to put it away. "We've got cameras."

"Relax. I'm not robbing the place." He casually put the baggie in the glove compartment and closed it. "These places were made for the munchies."

I took off my headset to make sure no one else could listen and leaned across the window. "Where's Viv?"

"She's at home. Doing home-stuff. You know how her mom gets."

"I'm aware. But...."

"But what?"

"But no," I said.

He strummed his fingers on the steering wheel. "I'm thinking of breaking up with her." He said it like describing the weather.

I couldn't tell if he was serious or getting a rise out of me. "Who breaks up with their girlfriend right before prom?"

"Well, it's gonna happen some time or another. Better to pull the bandage off all at once, you know?"

This is exactly why I didn't date guys my own age. "It's a dick move."

"I never said I was a saint."

"She loves you, Nico."

He sang the old Tina Turner song, "*What's love got to do with it? What's love...but a second-hand emotion?*"

"If this is about what I think it's about, then I'd like to tell you: don't worry. You'll be going to the Promised Land soon."

He shook his head. "Some things are too little, too late."

"Why are you telling me this?"

He found my eyes. "You know why."

"She's your girlfriend."

"And your best friend," he parroted back. As if I needed reminding. As if I wasn't reminded every time I saw her with him.

"Which is exactly why I'm not hanging out with you after work."

"I'm thinking of telling her."

My heart stopped. Would he dare tell Viv? I'd do anything for him not to. Anything but repeat that mistake.

"I'm not getting what I want," he said. "You're not getting what you want. Only Viv's getting what she wants. Seems like two out of three people aren't getting what they want."

"Nico, I'm fine where I am."

"So, you're getting what you want?" When I didn't answer, he said, "With who?"

"With nobody. I'm fine by myself."

He sat listening to a song in his car, weirdness descending on us, as if this was the most awkward date in the world. "She thinks you don't like me."

"Sometimes I don't."

With roguish charm, he said, "Could've fooled me."

My intercom burst to life with an order. "Gotta go. Nico, please. Don't say anything."

He pulled out a quarter. "Call it." He flipped it in his car.

It was ridiculous, but I went along. "Heads."

The quarter landed on his wrist.

I asked, "What is it?"

He smiled and said before driving off, "Wouldn't you love to know?"

I thought how trapped I was; how my secret had spawned another. I could never tell Viv the truth about how her "perfect relationship" simply wasn't true.

Like a spigot turned off, the rain finally stopped. We'd huddled around each other for warmth. We were as close as we'd been since the crash, shoulder to shoulder, hip-to-hip, round in a circle. There was something comforting about feeling the closeness of their skin near mine. For a long time no one said anything. Beads of water dripped from our faces. The sounds of the jungle returned—monkeys in the distance, insects, and frogs—and I took in the scent of clean air, dark sky giving way to daylight.

I was beginning to feel as if we were being punished. If I could only find out why, I could shout the answer to the heavens and we would be saved. Maybe we were being made to suffer so that we would find *meaning*, a gift given only to those who walked so close to death that they came back embracing life with a joy and ferocity they never had before. All the angst and worrying in the hallways of high school would mean nothing. Not when compared with this.

I've learned my lesson. I swear I have. Can I go now?

Nothing happened. The jungle remained as apathetic as ever.

Molly still carried my cross-body bag on her shoulder, and my mind ping-ponged to Johannes' book, to the pages on the tree branches, to the message we'd written in sand.

"Oh, God." I thought I'd said it to myself, but they looked at me. "All our messages. My pages…." I shook my head. "Not with the storm."

No one said it aloud, but we were all thinking it: *no one knows where we are. No one will find us.*

Their reaction made me wish I'd never said anything at all. The fact that they didn't react at all scared me more. They were beyond hysterics, beyond numb.

Ryan whispered from his stretcher. "I'm sorry."

Derek wrenched his hands together, as if they were wet rags. "What'd you say?"

"I'm sorry."

"You're apologizing?" He laughed to himself. "What would've made a difference, a real difference, is if we went *upriver* when I said it the first time. I don't want to say I told you so, but…." He looked at all of us with steely anger. "I told all of you."

"No," said Viv. "This," and she reached for an idea. "This is just like a video game. Right before you level up you face the biggest challenge. The Boss Challenge. This is our Boss Level." She tapped Ryan. "Right, Ryan?"

Ryan said, half-heartedly, "Right."

"C'mon, Ryan! I'm being positive here. What do you say? Nothing can kill the human spirit. We'll life-hack this. We'll make it."

Her speech didn't seem to rouse anyone. If anything, we only sunk deeper into despair.

"A fire! Let's make a fire," Viv said. "They'll see us from the sky. The smoke will billow up in big clouds. They'll see us for sure." Her smile almost convinced me.

Derek looked at her as if contemplating someone who didn't speak English. "If I could've made a fire, don't you think I would've? I've got no matches, no lighter, no glasses, and everything here, if you haven't noticed, is wet."

"What about rubbing together two sticks? You must've done that."

He sighed. "That's a lot harder than it looks. Almost impossible. And that's in optimal conditions."

When Derek made no move to at least try and start a fire, Viv got up and searched the surrounding area. She pulled at a root. A moment later, she picked up a stick. Sitting down, she began furiously rubbing them together.

I knew nothing would happen, and yet I held out hope, a fantastical hope of a spark, a miracle, a godsend.

Viv rubbed and rubbed, flakes of bark came loose like tiny, brown orange zest. She rubbed so hard the stick broke. As an A student, she wasn't used to failing. She repeated the entire process: searching for sticks, rubbing them together, her face one of concentration, biting her lower lip, and then the expected failure. In a fit, she threw the root and stick on the ground. "Nico."

"What?"

She looked at him as if it was obvious. "Do something."

"Like what?"

"I don't know. *Something*."

He reached into his baggie, picking at the remaining bud, and swallowed a piece. Viv jumped up towards the bag, but Nico pulled it out of her reach. His eyes flared. "Don't ever do that again."

"Why? Do you *need* it?"

"It sure as hell helps."

The tight circle had broken. Derek got up to pee. Molly stretched. Viv and Nico peeled off and argued in subdued voices.

Ryan whispered. "They're going to leave me. I know it. They're going to leave."

I tried to reassure him. "No, they won't."

"They will. Know how I know?" He waited for me to respond. "I'd leave me."

"I won't leave you."

"Then you're dumb."

Was I? "I won't let another person die."

"We're in the animal kingdom. Different rules. Different code. What would your poets say to that?"

I got up and approached Derek. I wrung out the wetness from my shirt and pants where I could. "Ryan thinks we're leaving him. Tell him it's not true."

Derek glanced at Ryan's body, splayed out on the ground. "Em, I know you don't want to hear this, but every day we sit here waiting for him to get better is a day wasted."

"I know."

"Good. Then it's decided."

"Nothing's decided. I'm not leaving him."

Derek looked at me strangely. "Why do you care?"

"Let's give him one day to rest. One day for all of us to rest."

"One day could mean the difference between life and death."

"I'm betting on life," I said.

"So am I." He pulled away from me.

"Then let's take a vote."

"A vote it is." He waved over Molly, Nico and Viv. They formed a circle around us. "Emily wants to take a vote."

Nico asked, "About what?"

Derek pointed at Ryan. "He's not doing well. Might be malaria, might be something else. But I say we keep going and come back for him. There's no way we can carry him anymore. We don't have the strength. All in favor of moving on, raise your hand."

Derek raised his. Without hesitation, Molly followed. Nico knitted his eyebrows, and after a second, he raised his hand.

Viv couldn't believe his vote. "Nico?"

"We'll come back for him."

Derek counted our hands. "That's three to two. Majority rules."

"Wait," I said. "What about Ryan? Doesn't he get a vote? That'll make it three to three."

Molly said, "Don't I get two, then?" She placed her hands over her belly. "This isn't just about me anymore."

The five of us stood, the silence between us growing until Derek said, "Tomorrow morning we leave. No matter what. You understand, Emily? *No matter what.*"

CHAPTER FOURTEEN

After my shift at Burger King, I drove over to Viv's. It was late on a school night, and I was still wearing my uniform, but she wanted to show me something that couldn't wait. I toyed with what it could be, chewing on my fingernails—a habit I gave up in junior high—but had inexplicably returned. I felt their jagged ends as I gripped the steering wheel.

I pulled into her driveway, my muffler rattling, and did a double take. A figure was perched in a tree. Not a cat or raccoon: a *person*. They brought their legs up to try and hide. I flicked on my brights. The beam didn't go high enough, but the person now knew I'd seen him.

As I opened my car door, the figure jumped from the tree, landed on all fours and scrambled away, dashing behind Viv's yard and through a neighboring privacy hedge. Whoever it was disappeared into the night, though I could've sworn from his loping gait it was Derek. I'd seen the back of his head for hours on end at work, his rounded shoulders as if caving in, and it had to have been him.

I walked to the tree and looked up. It was an old towering maple that stood next to Viv's house. Whoever had rested on the upper branch had seen directly into her window, a window currently with the blinds open and the lights on. Must've seemed like a burlesque show from the outside.

I went to the door and rang the bell. A melodious tone echoed inside. A minute later, Viv met me wearing Hello Kitty pajamas, her hair wet, and motioned me inside. "You came!" I thought there'd been an emergency. Her happiness threw me off. Inside, the foyer was laid with white marble, and I followed Viv up the stairs. My hand sliding up the carved banister, I walked past photos of her family—mother, father, Viv and an older sister already away in college. Going up the stairs was like moving through time. At the bottom Viv was a baby, and she grew older as the stairs ascended, from skiing trips to her standing in front of the Eiffel Tower and Big Ben.

I'd been here many times and was thankful not to have the usual interrogation disguised as conversation from Viv's mom. "Where are your parents?"

"Date night."

"Parents really do that?"

"Mine do. Not every week, but every month."

I couldn't fathom having a "family," let alone one where parents actually loved each other.

At the top of the stairs, we reached Viv's current age on the wall of photos from a recent trip they took to Lake Tahoe. We turned left down the hall and into her room. When I went to college, at least I knew I'd probably have a better dorm room than my own room. It would be an upgrade, and I would adapt well to living away from home. Viv, I thought, not so much. No dorm room could match the amenities she had here: an oversized room with her own en suite bathroom, a Queen-size sleigh bed, dark wood flooring, and triple-paned windows which kept the place draft-free and nearly soundproof. I admit, I was jealous. Her room, like her life, was protected, provided for, and mapped out on a road of seemingly rising steps to bigger and better things. Mine, not so much. Yet walking into her room felt as if I was being welcomed into a secret society, no matter my pedigree.

I went to her window and looked out onto the maple tree. "What were you doing a few minutes ago, before I came over?"

She opened the door to her walk-in closet. "Just got out of the shower. Why?"

I closed the blinds. "I think you had a Peeping Tom."

"Really?" She seemed both surprised and flattered. She rushed to the window and looked through the slats. "Where?"

I pointed at the maple outside her window, a tree that would give me nightmares. The type of tree I imagined that would come to life, shatter the windows and kidnap me to some cruel underworld.

She peered over the lawn, as if she would find a trace of who it was. "Did you see them?"

"Yes and no. I couldn't tell." I wasn't going to finger Derek if I wasn't 100% sure.

"Well, who do you think it was? A boy? An old man? A serial killer?"

"I don't know," I lied. "Someone our age by the looks of him."

"So you saw him."

"I saw his back." Viv waited for me to elaborate. "Viv, I saw a blur. That's it."

She kept looking out the window. Not scared. More *intrigued*.

"Aren't you going to call the police?"

"And tell them what? It'll just freak out my parents. My mom'll put me in lockdown if she thinks I have a stalker."

"Maybe you do."

"I don't think so. Climbing trees seems so…."

"Gross?"

"Innocent," Viv said. "Somehow sweet." She saw my face and explained. "I mean, if we're talking some creeper, yeah. But if it's a cute guy from school…."

"Unless he's out there recording you."

"Ew. Now that you put it that way…." She double-checked that the window lock was latched and flattened the slats.

I sat on her comfy bed, the kind where you could jump and jump and it wouldn't move, careful not to rub any of my grease stains on it. "So, what'd you want to show me that was so important?"

She went into her closet and with a theatrical "ta-da" pulled out her prom dress. "What do you think? It's Jovani."

It was beautiful. It had a high leg slit and a ruched bodice. Viv twirled with it in her room and went off on its details. "Feel the fabric. Like a cloud, right? And how great will my butt look in this? I thought of going with cream, but I went with red at the last minute. Impulse! Tell me you like it!"

We were so different, but she needed my approval as much as I needed hers. "You're gonna look like a movie star." I hadn't even bought my dress; I was going to look at second-hand shops. "You're still going with Nico, right?"

"Of course. I got him a color-coordinated tie."

Viv proceeded to tell me the story of choosing dresses, and the decision was as fraught as if she were shopping for a wedding dress. Colors, shapes, styles. Near misses, drama with a capital D. She wanted to make sure no one else would show up in it.

As she spoke, I zoned out, still wondering about Derek, if it was indeed him looking inside, and how it seemed odd that Viv wasn't more upset. It was as if she *knew* someone was outside; as if it happened regularly and she enjoyed the attention.

She could have her secrets and I could have mine.

Or maybe I was over-thinking the whole thing. She was so happy; giggling after every sentence, wanting to share her joy, bouncing on her feet, that's why she insisted I come over and why it couldn't wait. She really was like Beauty, swaying on the ballroom floor that was her bedroom, which by definition made me The Beast.

She offered me the dress. "Hold it up. See what it would look like on you."

I was a member of her club. I would be a sister to her. I met her warm smile with my own.

"I'd love to."

Ryan's face took on a sallow, yellow color. I wasn't sure what was wrong, but I knew it wasn't food poisoning. I'd had food poisoning once after eating a batch of clam chowder at some beach shack years ago and the sickness was vicious, like *I want to die* vicious. I still can't stomach the scent of clam chowder. But even in the throes of my misery, I never looked like this. I was never yellow. If Ryan kept going the way he was going, he'd turn Oompa-Loompa orange.

"One day they'll regret it," Ryan whispered, talking to no one. He lay on the ground, his head resting on a mound of dirt. "Got 'em hanging on my wall."

I knelt next to him. His pupils were constricted, small back dots surrounded by white. His breath was more a wheeze than anything else. "Who do you have hanging on the wall?"

"They remind me."

I asked again. "Who do you have hanging on the wall?" He'd fallen into a fever, and I wiped his forehead with the arm fabric from my shirt.

"Rejection letters."

College rejection letters, I thought. He hangs his college rejection letters on his wall. To keep him motivated. Seemed like torture. A kind of *Longing For What Never Came* in a different form.

"They'll regret it," he said.

"They will," I whispered. "They will."

I hoped the fever would break by morning. At the very least, I hoped his fever dreams sent him someplace far from here.

I got up and walked a few feet over to Molly, Viv, and Derek, who were busy building beds. "Do you feed a cold and starve a fever? Or is it the other way around?"

"Neither," Derek said. "Starving's never an answer for anything."

"Ryan should eat."

"We all should," Derek said and looked at the sky. "Too late to forage. Dark's coming."

I pointed at the cross-body bag around Molly's chest. "Then we'll eat the leftover popcorn." *Popcorn* seemed a more appetizing word than the real thing.

Derek said, "Why don't you grab Nico? Let us finish making the beds, and then we'll eat."

I asked Viv, "Where is he?"

She pointed and said, her face tight, "Being a jerk."

"Good to know," and I peeled off to find him. I walked into the wall of green, careful not to go far. Too many steps away from a visual marker were akin to an ocean tide washing away your footprints and with it your sense of direction. Up ahead I saw Nico, I thought, relieving himself near a tree. Then I saw his hand rapidly moving back and forth, and I realized with a start that he was doing something else. Something private.

I looked away. Embarrassed. Curious.

I stepped back and a branch cracked under my foot. Hearing it, his head spun, and a look of horror spread across his face. He stopped, flipping up his pants, and for a moment I thought he might run into the jungle out of shame. Seconds passed and he walked towards me, not meeting my eyes.

He got to me and said, "Please don't tell anyone."

"I don't know what you're talking about."

He appreciated the lie, nodding. "I just wanted to feel good, you know? I needed a moment of forgetting I was here."

"Like I said, I don't know what you're talking about." We could all use a moment of pleasure, even shared pleasure if we had the strength or interest.

Nico changed the subject. "Viv is driving me a little crazy."

"I gathered." I tried to make a joke. "I'm sure it's mutual."

"This...." He motioned to the jungle around us. "It changes things. Changes everything. Or maybe it didn't change anything at all. Just made me finally *see*."

"It'll all go back to normal when we get home."

"That's just it. I don't want it to go back to normal."

We took in the sounds of the jungle. The incessant buzz of insects had become a kind of sonic Chinese water torture. Suddenly, he lunged forward and kissed me.

I pushed him away. "What are you doing?"

He looked like a scolded little kid. "You ever think about that night?"

"No," I lied. "I never do."

"I do. All the time."

"It was a mistake." I hated that I had no one else to blame but myself.

"You got me wrong, Em. It's not just about that night. It's what could've been. You're fun. You read. You think about things. Viv," he sighed. "She's great and all. But she's not you."

I didn't know what to say; there really wasn't anything *to* say.

Nico said, "I've been doing things for other people. Trying to make them happy. 'Bout time I did things for me."

"Like what?"

He was about to speak when from beyond the jungle, we heard: "You bitch!"

Nico and I looked at each other. Had we heard it right? We paused, unsure, until we heard it again. "You fat bitch!" It was Viv's voice.

We ran.

Rounding a tree, we saw Viv holding the cross-body bag. She stood, pointing an accusatory finger at Molly.

I yelled, "What's wrong?"

"It's gone. The food. The grubs. Gone!" To prove it, Viv showed us the empty bag, turning it upside down. Gravy-like goo dripped from what little remained.

Molly shook her head, seemingly as shocked as we were. "I didn't eat them."

"Then who did? You were the only one who could have!"

"I swear I didn't eat them."

"Then how come they're gone? They didn't just slink out on their own."

Molly was on the verge of tears. "I'm hungry, too. I didn't. I swear I didn't."

Somehow we found ourselves on one side—Nico, Viv, Derek, me; and Molly on the other, an unconscious firing squad.

Nico tried to keep things calm. "Molly, was the bag ever out of your sight?" When she didn't answer, he asked again.

"No! It was never out of my sight. I wore it across my chest. I don't know what happened. I don't know how...." She reached for an explanation. "Maybe they fell out."

This time, it was Viv who rolled her eyes.

"Maybe while walking, the bag went sideways, and the grubs slipped out."

Her explanation didn't ring true.

Molly pointed at Viv and me. "They never liked me. Viv and her shadow, and Nico, of course he's gonna side with them." She turned to Derek. "But you believe me, right? You know what it's like to have everyone against you...."

Derek didn't answer.

"Derek, you have to believe me."

Anger rose in me. Earlier she'd implied that I would steal the food. It took a lot of work to get those grubs. It'd helped our morale just knowing there *was* food, and now it was gone.

Molly sensed our disbelief. Fear radiated off of her in waves. Maybe she thought we'd abandon her. "I didn't take it!" Molly stuck her finger down her throat. "I'll prove it!" She pushed her finger to the back of her mouth, wiggling, retching.

"Stop it!" Nico grabbed her hand. "It won't prove anything. You either didn't eat 'em, or if you did—"

"I didn't!"

"Then it's probably already digested." Nico turned to us. "This isn't helping. What's done is done."

Viv asked, "What are you saying?"

"We forget it and move on."

"That was our food, Nico. Our food."

"We'll get more."

"Not until morning," said Derek.

Nico glanced at the darkening sky. "Then we're just gonna have to wait."

As if on cue, my stomach rumbled. It took a few seconds for us to realize nothing was going to change. No amount of accusations or arguing was going to make food suddenly appear.

We split off to finish our beds, our movements lagging, saving our energy. Later I heard Molly crying and I wondered if it was because she'd been caught, or whether she'd been telling the truth. That was worse to consider. Because if she didn't steal it, then who the hell did?

CHAPTER FIFTEEN

"Hush, little baby, don't say a word, Mama's gonna buy you a mockingbird. If that mocking bird won't sing, Mama's gonna buy you a diamond ring."

I open my eyes. My mother is leaning over me, softly singing a nursery rhyme. I've never heard her sing before, and it's pretty. Soothing. I like this version of my mom.

"If that diamond ring turns to brass, Mama's gonna buy you a looking glass." When her eyes meet mine, I can see the haze behind them. She's had Ativan—at least two, maybe more—and she's in one of her fuzzy states. The nursery rhyme isn't so pleasant anymore, and I can smell the antiseptic cleaner the hospital uses.

"Did I ever tell you how much I love you?" she asks.

If I was home I could just walk away. Here, I'm a captive audience. Stuck.

Her voice takes on that dreamy quality I'm all too familiar with. "So many times I thought to myself: what if? What if I wasn't a mother? What if I never moved out here? What if I could start all over? To be your age again." She smiled ruefully. "The things I'd do differently. You don't have those thoughts. Not at your age. But you will. One day, we all have those thoughts."

"Mom, I'm tired," I lie.

She takes no heed. "I've thought so many things. Possibilities." Her eyes land on mine. "If I never had you."

"Mom, please."

"No," and she reaches out and holds my hand. Her grip is strong, almost crushing. "You need to hear this. You need to know." Her eyes are haggard, and I realize she's been crying. "When I got that phone call and the man told me there'd been a crash, I hung up. I hung up and stared at the phone and prayed it wouldn't ring. You don't know what those seconds felt like." Her body tenses, as if holding something within, afraid to let it out. "When the phone rang again, I unplugged it. The apartment got quiet and I thought *can't reach me now, can you?* And then my cell phone rang, and that's when I knew. I knew my baby was gone."

She stops herself from falling apart. "I thought of all the things I'd wished for, my selfish thoughts floating around, caught in the clouds, just waiting…." Her mouth trembles. "And your plane flew right into them."

I consider pressing the nurse's button to get her to stop.

"It's my fault, Emily. If I'd never thought those things, if I'd never…. Some wishes almost came true, don't you see?" The dam bursts and she cries, a wounded animal next to my bed. She buries her head in my quilt, my mother reduced to a little girl, a parishioner to my priest. "I don't wish them anymore. I don't wish for anything but you." She lifts her head. "Can you forgive me? Can you ever forgive me?"

I look into her eyes.

She waits for my answer.

CHAPTER SIXTEEN

That night in the jungle I dreamt of food—red ripe cherries hanging from a tree. I anticipated biting into one, juice dribbling down my chin. I reached up to a branch and it was too high. The cherries were so close and their sweet scent only stirred my hunger. I scrambled up the tree, and as I did, the tree seemed to expand. For every step I climbed, the branches stretched above me, telescoping into the sky. I climbed; they stretched. The tree grew so tall that I was in the clouds. Looking down, there was nothing but vast empty space and the pattern of the earth. I pushed one last time and jumped to a branch and grabbed onto it, my body hanging loose, feet swaying beneath me. I inched over and picked off a cherry.

I was about to pop it in my mouth when I heard the sharp crack of a branch and it snapped.

I fell in my dream.

I didn't want to die in a dream.

I didn't want to die.

Someone else, but not me.

I slammed into the earth and woke with a shudder. The tartness of the phantom cherry rested on my lips. I was left with my hunger pains and I moaned, or I thought I did, only to confuse the sound with Ryan's labored breathing. I crawled out of my bed, moving in the dark, and slid into his. His body was furnace hot. I snuggled close, spooning him. If he died in the night, he wouldn't be alone. Having a body next to me made me feel less lonely, too. Ryan whispered gibberish and I gently shushed him, brushing my hand over his head.

"Sleep, Ryan. Sleep."

We did. We slept.

In the morning, I opened my eyes and Ryan was facing me. For a moment, I thought he might be dead, for his eyes stayed unblinkingly on mine. Then he said, his voice weak, "How long have you been here?"

It was the first thing he said that had made sense in the last 24 hours. I reached out and felt his forehead. I touched again to be sure. "Your fever. It broke." His jaundice, too, didn't seem as severe. "How do you feel?"

"Like shit, but I'll live."

He rolled to get out of the bed, and I placed my hand on him. "Rest. You'll need it."

I got up and woke everyone up, sharing the good news. They seemed relieved. No one had to make the impossible choice. If I was honest with myself, I was relieved, too. Before the moment of truth, it was easy to say, of course, I would stay with Ryan. Of course I wouldn't leave him. But if the moment really came, I wasn't so sure. I hated that seed of doubt.

The first thing we needed was food. I was hungry. It went beyond sensation. It was *need*, like an addict seeking his next hit. Everything revolved around filling that need, every thought, every action.

We left Ryan behind, and he seemed peaceful lying in the bed, caught in a tableau of mist, almost otherworldly. He Zen-ed out in Nature's Garden while we split off in search of fruit, creating new finger-like paths in the green.

No one spoke. The jungle's varied vocabulary filled the emptiness.

I'd read about Japanese soldiers, lost in a jungle during World War II, who continued to fight for months or years after the war ended because they were cut off from civilization. It had only been a few days, and I had the feeling anything could've happened in our absence. Catastrophes, terrorism, nuclear war. Why else would it take rescuers so long to find us?

I tried to keep my thoughts positive: *You'll be fine. They'll find you.*

No, a voice argued, the plane might be lost.

They'll find the black box.

What if the black box was damaged?

Impossible.

Nothing's impossible. You know that.

Above me, a weird-looking black monkey with a white furry face ate fruit. He hopped along the treetops, picking at dark, round berries. If it was good enough for a monkey, it was good enough for me. Unlike my dream, I easily grabbed onto the tree and climbed, finding purchase on branches, one branch and then another, careful to avoid strange bugs, until I picked a bunch of berries. Perched in a tree, I yelled for Derek.

A moment later, he emerged and looked up at me. Out of all of us, Derek seemed the most in his element. His upbeat mood made me wonder if it wasn't him who had stolen the food.

I tossed down a few berries. "What do you think?"

Catching them, he rubbed one against his lips, not eating. He waited, then cringed and dropped them. "No bueno."

I held the berries in my hand. They looked delicious. "What do you mean no good?"

"My lips are tingling. They're poisonous."

"But I saw a monkey eating them."

"Em, it's evolution. They live here, we don't."

I climbed down the tree and met him at the bottom. "What about you? Any luck?"

He shook his head.

The more I looked, the more berries I saw. They were everywhere: on trees and bushes, and all of them forbidden. How long would it take before we crushed them in our mouths for lack of anything else?

Derek and I inched along, our eyes peeled. Green and brown gave way to more green and brown.

"Would you have really left Ryan?"

He didn't even look up. "The needs of the many outweigh the needs of the few. Or the one."

"This isn't Star Trek."

"It's the principal."

"And I could recite another one," I said. "Leave no man behind."

"Clearly," Derek motioned toward his thin physique and said, "I'm not a military man." He saw how I looked at him. "Don't judge, Em. This stopped being a high school trip as soon as we hit the water. You can throw stones once we're back under four walls and a roof. Until then, it's survival." He leaned in. "And if you want to live, you'll follow my lead."

We searched for another ten minutes when we heard screams. Ryan's voice pierced through the jungle, much worse than when he was bitten by ants. They weren't screams of pain or frustration; they were *something else*. They were the screams before falling into the abyss.

Derek burst ahead of me.

I followed and ran back through the tangled vines, seemingly lost in a dark fairy tale.

I emerged into the clearing where we'd built our bamboo beds. Ryan's screams filled the air, and along with it, a curious fast rustling. Viv, Nico, Molly and Derek had beaten me there and stood in a semi-circle far on the outskirts. All I saw were their backs. Whatever they were watching had frozen them in place.

"What's wrong?" I yelled, but they didn't turn. Didn't speak. Didn't move.

With tentative steps, I approached them in my own personal horror film, fearful of what I would find, and when I did, I understood.

A blur of black, a flash of white, and Ryan on the ground.

A wild boar charged Ryan. The boar moved like thunder, a hideous creature of black bristled hair and tusks. It had gored Ryan, lifting him off the bamboo bed and dropped him on the flat surface. Ryan screamed, his mouth releasing a horrible sound, a note of despair and fear, that for all his challenges, this beast next to him was one he could not overcome.

He was alone. A gladiator of one.

His chest bled from the wounds, flaccid flesh surrounding leaking holes.

He lay, tired and shocked, but not defeated. I saw his mouth move, and imagined him saying, "Help me." He began crawling—crawling towards us. As he did, the semi-circle moved away.

I was paralyzed with fear. Any second, the creature could attack us. But Ryan was the easier prey.

The boar charged, and Ryan tried to dodge it, splaying flat and eating mud, but the boar raked his tusks into the ground. The tusks caught Ryan in the back, impaling him. Ryan's body went rigid. Red spilled onto the white ivory and the beast lifted Ryan like he was nothing at all, like a terrier shaking a toy.

I couldn't look any longer.

I couldn't look at my friends doing nothing.

I picked up a piece of broken bamboo and ran at the boar. "No!" I yelled and swung the bamboo over the boar's head. With a hollow thud, it bounced harmlessly off.

The boar faced me, its eyes little slits, releasing angry, guttural growls.

How I hated that creature.

I took the bamboo pole with the V-groove, using it like a spear, and I charged.

Damn this jungle, I thought. Damn this death.

The bamboo hit the pig, and the laws of physics played themselves on in that clearing, where its weight held it steady, but launched me to the side, and I fell into the mud. The boar's thick hide had protected it.

But I had certainly pissed it off.

It bared its mouth, releasing a breath of foul air.

Fear gave way to survival. I grabbed the bamboo and thrust at its face, again and again. The boar kicked up dirt, scuttling back and forth holding its piece of property, and every second felt far too long. My mind was empty. My vision tunneled, and all that existed, had ever existed and ever would, was the boar and I.

I jammed the bamboo into its snout. With a squeal, it gave up and scurried off into the jungle, darting away.

Time kicked into gear.

To my right, Molly, Viv, Nico and Derek stood watching, caught in a chrysalis between what had happened and what was yet to come. They hadn't moved. They hadn't done anything.

Cowards.

I turned to Ryan to tell him it was all right, we'd saved him, we would bandage his wounds, and it would be a great story to tell one day.

But he was still.

Too still.

His eyes opened to the sky, his face contorted in confusion, as if asking *why me, why me?*

CHAPTER SEVENTEEN

The mud was saturated with water and could absorb nothing more, so Ryan's blood floated on top like a cartoonish oil slick. We stood over him and he looked like a boy, smaller in death than the image we carried in our memories. Lying there, his body seemed such a fragile vessel for such a resilient spirit.

The boar had attacked Ryan because he was weak. Because Ryan had been near death. I wondered if we were all near death, reeking of it from our pores and not knowing, having grown used to the smell.

I didn't know what to call Ryan's demise. Accidental death? Murder? I wanted it to be something classifiable, something with resonance. Otherwise, his passing in time would become a joke, yet another story about "When Animals Attack," or some anecdote kids would throw around at parties. ("Hey, you hear about the guy who got gored? That's some sick shit, man.") I'm not even sure what killed him: the boar, the jungle, or the rest of us who didn't lift a finger to help.

Ryan could've been saved. Should've been saved. I turned to them. "We should never have left him alone."

Derek said, "What's done is done, Em. It was a mistake. It happened. There's nothing we can do."

"He didn't need to die." None of them met my face except Derek.

"I refuse to feel guilty," he said. "And I don't."

I looked at the rest of them. "Do any of you?" When none of them answered, I said, "I thought you didn't do anything because you were scared. At least that I could understand. But if you did nothing because you *chose not to*?" They looked anywhere but at me.

"I told you," Derek said. "It's survival. So before you get on your high horse, think this through."

"He's dead. Ryan's dead."

"What if the boar gored one of us? What then? Who would carry 'em? There's no 911, no ambulance, no hospital. There's only putting one foot in front of the other, and praying you don't fall sick, or slip and break a bone because there's no room for error. No safety net. Nothing but ourselves."

There it was: cold logic. I didn't want to be logical. I wanted to be right. "I think you let him die."

"What?"

The answer was like a bolt of truth. "You let him die. To save your energy. To not have to share food. To save yourselves. He was slowing us down. Sapping our strength because we had to carry him. He was dead weight to you."

Derek turned away.

"Where do you think you're going?"

"I'm not gonna stay here and listen to this. I'm hungry. And if I find enough food, I'll bring enough for all of us."

"What about Ryan? We can't just leave him out here in the open! The animals will get him."

"They'll get him anyway! Whether we dig him deep or not."

The others were starting to split off. Viv said, "He's right, Em."

"Can we at least say a few words? Before we leave him?" Before we leave him forever, I thought. I picked up a few large leaves, the closest thing to a funeral sheet I could think of and laid them over Ryan's body.

How fast would it take the jungle to erase his very presence? I wondered if we'd ever be able to find him again. At his funeral back home there might be a casket, but no body or bones inside, only an empty space.

The group paused, waiting for one of them to make the decision, and then the rest would follow. Derek walked forward. Viv, Nico and Molly circled around Ryan, hands at their sides. We bowed our heads. I pictured soft shafts of light falling through the canopy on him, and whether it was true or not, that's how I was always going to remember it.

Viv said, "Does anyone know what to say?"

"Goodbye, Ryan," I said. "You helped save us."

Derek scoffed.

"Rest in peace." I looked at the others. "Anyone else?"

Nico said, simply, "Be well."

Nico gazed at Viv and she shook her head, declining to say anything.

Molly said, "I don't know why you were so mean. Someone told me that hurt people hurt people. Maybe you were one of those. I'm glad you don't hurt anymore."

Silence fell over us, and Derek was the last to speak.

"He was a douche." He looked at me. "Satisfied?"

We moved downriver. We'd come too far to turn around and head all the way back to the crash site. I hated to admit it, but we traveled faster without Ryan, and though the jungle never got any easier to traverse, we picked up a rhythm, a sense of where to step and where to avoid which increased our tempo.

Derek took the leadership position. There was no discussion; it just happened. He used his metal makeshift hatchet to whack down the overgrowth, and as he did, I sensed a change in him. Like watching when the President takes the oath of office. Something happens when they place their hand on a bible and swear to protect the country from all enemies, foreign and domestic. Seriousness descends upon them. Derek had that same seriousness; he was in charge now, something he probably never experienced before. He commanded and carried a certain respect.

I walked behind him. He caught my eye. "I know what you're thinking."

"No, you don't."

"I don't know where that idea came from that you can't speak ill of the dead. As if dying somehow erases what people did while they were alive."

"I didn't say anything, Derek."

"But you're thinking it, Emily. I know you. I can see it. I held my tongue back there. But I'll tell you what I really wanted to say: I'm not sorry he's dead. He was a bully. Life just got a whole lot better. Not just for me. For all the people from this moment on who won't ever cross paths with him."

"You don't know that. He could've changed."

"No one changes. Not really. People say they do, but I don't believe it. I'll always be what I've always been."

"And what's that?"

He considered and smirked. "King of the World."

Maybe the plane crash was the best thing to have ever happened to Derek Wert. How messed up was that?

"What's that make me?" I asked.

"I don't know. What *does* it make you?"

Not you, I thought. Definitely not you.

Still hungry, my body felt as if it was eating itself. There was a black hole in my stomach and it sucked everything into it. I knew I could live without eating for a few days, but my body let me know in no uncertain terms it would make me pay; it would remind me with every step, kicking and screaming like a baby's cry, I want food!

Up ahead white mushrooms dotted the jungle floor like edible Whack-a-Moles. They were shaped like little umbrellas. I was so giddy at the sight, I shouted, "Food! Food!" Saliva gathered in my mouth. I reached down and picked their caps, about to eat them, when Derek grabbed my hands and scolded, "No!"

He took them from my hands and rubbed the mushrooms together, effectively crumpling them up.

The others had come running.

"Why did you do that?" I said.

"Why do you think? They're poisonous. Like, deadly."

I stared down at them. "But they're the same kind you gave Ryan."

Molly, Viv, and Nico looked at Derek. Feeling their gaze, he said, "There's all kinds of mushrooms, Em. A lot of them look alike. Some look just like that one, but they're a shade whiter."

My stomach rumbled, and my thinking was cloudy from hunger, but I was certain those were the mushrooms Ryan had eaten. The same ones that nearly killed him.

Derek added, "I didn't like the guy, that's no secret. But come on." Derek didn't wait to engage in a debate, and he continued onward, the matter settled. I found Viv's face, and though we didn't say anything, she seemed to ask me *what does it matter now?*

As Molly and Nico walked past, I grabbed ahold of Viv and whispered. "Those were the mushrooms."

"You really believe Derek poisoned him on purpose?"

I didn't say it aloud for I feared the answer would make it real. Once spoken, there was no way to backtrack. But in my heart, I knew: Derek had gotten his revenge.

CHAPTER EIGHTEEN

The camera flash nearly blinded me. I wore a second-hand rose-colored dress I'd found at Goodwill. (The Goodwill located near Beverly Hills always had fantastic cast-offs.) Derek stood next to me in a fitted tuxedo, his hand hovering close to my rib cage in an embrace. With each successive photo, his hand grew firmer and more squirrely.

"Smile," Miranda said.

I smiled, showing my slightly crooked teeth, which never had braces.

"Perfect," she said.

Miranda and Derek's father stood off to the side of their living room. I caught his father's eyes on my legs, subtly checking me out. He had a cocktail in his hand and its bourbon-y smell wafted through the room. He looked how I felt: here only because of the person next to him.

"Give her the corsage, honey."

The whole picture-taking event seemed choreographed and scripted by Derek's mother, and we followed along, dutiful actors playing a part. Derek slid a wrist corsage on me and I did the honors of pinning one against his lapel. Derek would've looked dapper if he wasn't so nervous and had better posture. Derek, I realized, with all of his economic advantages, probably wished to have been born anyone else but himself.

"One last picture," Miranda said. "Give her a kiss."

My mortification complete, Derek leaned into my cheek and left a wet smear.

"That is just adorable!"

I know Miranda drove Derek nuts. She was the very definition of a helicopter parent, but I thought it must be nice to have someone who, you know, gave a damn. The whole event was the exact opposite from my home. My mother didn't know I was going to prom, and she didn't ask when I took longer in the bathroom to do up my hair. I could've told her, I suppose. That would've been the mature thing. But I wanted *her* to make the effort. That would've been the proper mom-thing. Or maybe I was just scared of another trip to the Olive Garden to talk about dating and sex.

Once outside, we took another photo with the limousine as our backdrop, and Miranda hugged me. She whispered, "Have a good time tonight. I hope it's *magical*." She slid a small envelope into my purse.

We got into the limo, all smiles, and as soon as the chauffeur closed the door, I let my face settle into repose. I could feel the muscles slacken, tired from all the false smiles.

Derek said, "Thanks for doing that, Em. I don't know how I can pay you back."

I opened my silver purse and took out the envelope and ran my finger under the glue. "Your mother, ohmygod. She gave me this." I laughed and showed it to him.

It was a room key from the same hotel where our prom was being held. The room was probably strewn with roses and champagne, complete with a couples massage and breakfast in bed.

Derek said, "Now you know why I am the way I am."

"It's sweet. Maybe it's in case you drink too much."

"That's what this is for," and he pointed at the limo.

"It's like those honeymoon suites from *The Bachelor*. They don't always have sex, you know."

He considered and looked over at me hopefully. "I'd hate for the room to go to waste."

I shook my head, the meaning clear: not gonna happen. No way, no how.

"Guy's gotta try," and he smiled.

We pulled up to a five star hotel. A line of limos parked nearby—stretch limos, massive SUV limos, and the mother of all ostentatious ones had a hot tub in the back. Other kids had borrowed their parents' cars. My favorite was an old-time-y car with a crank that reminded me of Charlie Chaplin. Maybe they were rented from a specialty car place, but I thought not: they were from some father's car collection. Girls I recognized from school paraded past in designer gowns, gloriously dressed and sparkling, bright with promise and I was struck with how much I would've liked to have gone with Johannes. It was, of course, impossible, but it didn't stop me from dreaming.

I always felt prom was one of those overrated high school conventions that people put too much importance on, like New Year's Eve parties with all the pressure to have the best time ever and were inevitably a disappointment. The best times came from the unexpected, the unplanned.

And yet, my DNA couldn't resist being part of something elegant, something so red-carpety. I wasn't Jewish or Hispanic or southern and would never have a Bat Mitzvah, Quinceanera or cotillion ball. Aside from some far-off (potential) wedding, this is the closest I'd get to feeling like, well, not a princess, but someone pretty. Someone special.

When I'd first told Viv I was going to prom with Derek she thought I was joking. She didn't believe me, not for days. When she realized I wasn't joking, her perpetual smile fell to a concerned grimace, and then back to normal. "You could always come with us!"

There were facts: I couldn't go with the man I wanted. I didn't want to go alone. And as much as Viv insisted we'd have fun, there was no way I was going to take the spotlight away from Viv's night. She *loved* prom, had probably planned for it since elementary school. In the end, I told her no.

Once inside, prom was prom: the decked-out ballroom. The 10-piece live band complete with back-up singers that played a variety of jazz, classics, ballads and occasional covers. I gazed over the students and had fun determining who was either bored, having a horrible date, or in love. Of course, no school dance was without The Spectacle. Like clockwork there was a couple arguing, a girl soon to be in tears, a gaggle of her friends trying to calm her down.

But what took the cake was the horrible activity called dancing. No twerking allowed. No "freak" dancing. Still: there was enough overbite and awkwardness to last a lifetime. Education taught us many things but rarely the necessities on how to survive in life and dating.

Off to the side, Johannes watched it all, snazzy in his tux. Next to me, Derek stood and offered his arm.

On the dance floor, it killed me to be so close to Johannes. I'd caught his eye as he watched me dance and I imagined him as my date, twirling me on the dance floor, his lips nuzzling my neck. Instead, Derek stepped on my feet and proceeded to sweat as he placed his hands on my back, his body as firm as a wet noodle.

Derek asked, "How am I doing?"

I tried not to clench my teeth. "Good. You're doing good."

"This is my first time dancing."

"Really? You'd never know."

He caught me looking off to the sidelines. "Who are you looking at?"

I didn't think I was being so obvious. "Oh, nothing."

"You're like a chick from a spy film doing the Tango. Are you hiding some moves? Karate chops? A gun under your dress?"

"Nothing like that," I said. "Though I am an assassin."

Though Derek was nervous, he seemed to be having a good time. Underneath his awkwardness, this was who he really was. Not a bad guy, I thought.

I felt good about myself. I was doing a good thing. I'd made Derek happy, and in doing so, I was happy. At least he was trying and I spent a few more dances on the floor until my toes couldn't take anymore.

I took a bathroom break, hoping Johannes would follow. I thought he'd find me in the hotel hallway, but he never did. He was the chaperone. It was a school event. And dancing with a student was *verboten*. I wasn't looking for anything illicit, only romantic. A gesture. A rose. Something.

I got a lot of strange glances from my classmates wondering what Derek and I were doing together. On the way back to the table, I overheard someone ask, "Did she lose a bet or something?" I was thankful Derek wasn't in earshot. No lost bet. Like "It's A Wonderful Life", I was earning my wings.

I sat back at the table with Derek, watching Viv and Nico, arms entwined, a smile on her face, boredom on his. They were together. My secret still held.

Even though I walked with a murderer, I didn't feel threatened. I didn't know what I planned to do when I got back, but Viv was right: what did it matter right now?

So when we came across a big batch of mushrooms and Derek deemed them safe, we piled our faces, shoveling them in. They tasted like earth and fiber, grit and grass. Taste didn't matter; sustenance did, and the satisfying feeling of fullness. So many things I had worried about fell away. Survival stripped away the nonsense of modern living. I vowed on my return to forgo shopping, to watch less TV, or get rid of it altogether; to live simply and wake with gratitude at being alive.

I made a list: be nicer to my mom, be an honest friend, help people more, and to think about myself less. The insistent *Me! Me! Me!* was a recipe for madness.

When we finished, our mouths little lawnmowers, we packed my cross-body bag so full of mushrooms the bag couldn't clamp shut. No one asked Molly if she would carry it. Viv suggested me, since it was my bag. I declined. I told Viv, "You should." Everyone trusted Viv.

Nico asked Derek, "Are any of these mushrooms the magic type?"

"Nope. Don't need you bugging out while we're trying to get out of here."

"I didn't mean for now. I meant, maybe I could take 'em back home." Off our looks, he said, "Something good should come from this trip."

Viv said, "Making it out alive is all I'm asking for."

Nico said, "Pretty basic, don't you think?"

"Sometimes you're so stupid, Nico."

"Look, we're getting out of here. That's not debatable. What worries me is when we get back."

Viv said, "Why?"

"Hasn't this experience made you think? Like, what are we doing, going to school, doing the things we do?"

"Are you stoned?"

"Stop asking me that!" Nico calmed down. "Can I just have a thought without you harping on me?"

Viv's face went tight. But she stayed put.

"I'm just saying," Nico continued, "we learn all this stuff and yet we don't know anything. Not really. I don't know how to survive. I couldn't hunt if my life depended on it. I can't read the stars. I don't know a poisonous beetle from a ladybug. I can't even do math without a calculator. Can't spell without spellcheck."

"So what are you saying? You're gonna drop out of school? You're on the National Honor Society. You get straight As without trying."

"I know I'm smart. Learning things comes easy to me. I'm just wondering what I'm studying *for*...besides to make a living. 'Cause that seems pretty shallow from where I'm sitting."

"You could always stay," Viv said.

"I hate this place. And it probably hates me." He burped, waved it away and turned to us. "Forget I brought it up. In fact, your mission, should you choose to accept it, is to brainwash me back to commercialism with extreme prejudice. Once we get back I'll be the first in line to deforest this place. Hell, give me a bulldozer and I'll plow this place down."

Sadly, we all probably felt the same: we were splattered with mud, our arms crisscrossed with scratches, our skin polka-dotted with insect bites and scabs, and looking at Viv I thought I could Paint-by-Numbers across her body.

Suddenly, the buzz of insects went from a drone to white static, growing ever louder. It seemed to take shape, morphing around us, as if a swarm was approaching.

Viv raised her head to the sky. "Are there killer bees in the jungle?"

"No," Derek said.

Nico said, "The bugs are going nuts out here."

Derek tilted his head. "Those aren't bugs." He listened more intently, his lips curving into a smile. "It's a plane."

"A plane?" Molly asked.

Derek said, "It's coming this way."

Smiles spread across their faces. Not mine: I didn't want a repeat of the damn parrot. As we listened, it was clear, the sounds of a propeller, flying low. I wanted to cry.

Viv said, "They haven't forgotten about us!"

The canopy of trees blocked the view; there was no way a plane could see us. Derek said, "We've gotta get out in the open."

We ran towards the river. Cannibals could've been after us, and we wouldn't have run any faster. I leaped over a stump, tripped, and almost wiped out. I got back on my feet and pushed leaves and branches out of my way, running through them like solid cobwebs—

The plane was coming closer—

Nico passed me. Derek, too—

This was it. Our rescue! I was going home!

The plane was nearly overhead—

I burst out from the wall of green into the open and waded into the river, waving my hands overhead. I heard the sound of the plane's propeller fly past before I saw it: a small floatplane, the kind that could land on the water, its engine in the nose, a streak of yellow in the sky.

"Hey! Over here! Over here!"

We jumped up and down, trying to make ourselves bigger.

Desperate, I shouted to Nico. "Your watch!" The watch was silver and could reflect the sun. Nico slipped off his watch, adjusting it in the air to find the light.

"Hurry!"

It reflected.

But the plane soon looked like the silhouette of a giant mosquito, continuing its path down the river.

Viv and Molly screamed, "No! Turn back! Turn back! We're right here!"

"Just wait," Nico said. "It'll turn around."

Derek's head was down, his hands on his face. If he'd given up, there had to be a reason. "Derek?" I asked.

He hesitated, not wanting to break our spirits. "He would've dipped his wing."

"Not always, right?" said Nico. "Maybe they've got different rules down here. He didn't just fly right over us. He'd have to have seen us. He'd have to."

Derek didn't answer, only slowly waded back to shore.

We stayed in the river, waving our hands and holding out hope, with water up to our knees. We stupidly thought maybe the pilot had a rear-view mirror or a camera on the plane—like one of those weird Google mapping cars—that graphed and plotted our whereabouts and spit out the coordinates on a computer screen.

The buzzing grew more distant until it quieted completely and the plane flew out of view.

It seemed like a mirage; we'd seen it, and now the sky sat empty, a hellacious joke.

Here's hope, folks. Oops! My mistake!

We waited. The plane had to turn around sometime. We waited even though we saw Derek picking leeches from his legs. Even though we knew they were probably attaching to our skin, and the longer we waited, the more there would be. We waited, not wanting to move from that highway of air. If there had been one plane, wouldn't there be another?

We waited, letting our bladders empty, waited while we grew hungry again, waited while our skin pruned until by clear evidence the plane would never turn back.

CHAPTER NINETEEN

I walked into Johannes' classroom after the last bell of the day and closed the door behind me. Around the room, there was a ring of photos in black and white, all writers from Papa Hemingway, Joyce Carol Oates, Carl Sandburg, Gwendolyn Brooks, to Emily Dickinson. I could picture myself up there with them, a club of wordsmiths, not the most attractive of people, but as my mother might say, I would fit right in.

Johannes sat behind a desk, working on his computer. Seeing me, a smile spilled over his face and he said, "Em, what are you doing here?"

"Figured I'd come and see my favorite teacher."

Johannes rolled back in his chair and stood up. "You excited about the trip?"

"Can't wait."

He sensed I was holding something back. "What?"

"It's nothing."

"Uh oh," he said. "Spill."

"I know you're Mr. I've Been Everywhere, but I've never flown before. I've never left Southern California." I felt immature and inexperienced.

"There's no reason to. You're less than three hours away from everything. The beach, mountains, desert."

"It's not the travel. It's the plane. It freaks me out. It's, like, an aluminum death tube."

He laughed. "Planes freak me out, too. But when I hit turbulence, I like to think of what William Shakespeare would think, flying above the clouds, traveling faster than he could imagine. And then I consider myself lucky to endure a few bumps. But I'll try to keep the image of aluminum out of my head." He added, "I'm honored that I'll be with you for your maiden flight. In fact, there's a ritual for first-timers."

"Is not."

"Is, too." He playfully bopped my nose. "You get to make a wish. Like fallen eyelashes. When you're in the air, you make a wish. And it comes true because you're closer to heaven."

"You made it up."

"Google it." He swiveled and offered his laptop.

I knew it was a lie, but a cute one. "Have you made a wish?"

"Of course." He didn't elaborate.

"Well, what was it?"

"Can't tell you. Then the wish wouldn't come true."

"I guess," I said jokingly, "I wasn't your wish."

"No, I meant it's bad luck to talk about. Like birthday wishes."

"But not completely made-up traditions like first-time fliers?"

Johannes smiled. "Are we having our first fight?"

"Are we?" I teased.

He shrugged, the "fight" over. "That was easy." He walked across the room and opened the door. "You best get going, closed doors get people whispering."

"Why? Someone on your schedule?" I peeked into his notebook and saw the name. "Molly Higgins?" I picked up the work she'd turned in for class. A poem:

I see faces
and the race
to make
me a disgrace
Outcast, outside

oversized, ostracized
What side is fairness
What side is mercy
What side is love
Tell me
So I know where to stand

"You gave her an A. You only gave me a B+."

"You weren't supposed to see that. Besides, it's not about technique. It's the honesty in what she wrote. That's what gives it its power."

"Mine had power." I heard the whine in my voice and hated it.

"But it wasn't real. It was…reaching for the truth. Molly bled on the page and it shows."

I placed the poem back on his desk. There was a knock. It was Molly.

"Mr. DeKoning? We had a four o'clock?"

"We did. Ms. Duran was just leaving."

I walked past, sensing disappointment and sadness on Molly's face, which I thought was odd.

"Thanks for your help, Mr. D.," I said, purposely shortening his name, laying claim to him. "See you later." And I would. At his apartment.

Or so I thought.

Later, he cancelled; too many papers to grade. So he said.

In the hospital, a man who is not a doctor or a nurse enters my room. He wears a tailored suit, some kind of textured shoes that clack on the floor, and he has too bright teeth that contrast with his too tan face. I'd seen Hollywood types walking through the hallways of Riverdale, their progeny in tow as they toured the academy. This was my first experience up close. I wonder if he'd walked into the wrong room.

"Emily Duran, Alan White. But please call me Alan." Before I knew it, his hand appears and I'm shaking it.

"No one told me I had a visitor."

"Quite a trip you had, isn't it?" His voice is like velvet. "You mind?" He motions toward a chair. I nod and he sits down.

"Who are you?" I ask.

"I could give you my title, but really, I'm someone who can help you. You're at a very precarious place right now."

"I am?" I wonder if my mother set this up.

"An enviable one. Let me cut to the chase. Emily, may I call you that? A lot of outlets are chasing you, trying to get you on their talk shows, score interviews. But here's the thing. It's all about them. *Their* ratings. *Their* bragging rights. Someone needs to look out for *you*."

"Why me?" *I'm just Emily Duran.*

"They want your story."

I have an irrational fear that he is going to scoop up my laptop and run off with it.

"Some of these outlets are willing to pay, and pay handsomely. Without the right representation, you may not get your worth. What your *experience* is worth. What the lives of your friends are worth."

I'm about to speak, but he wags a finger.

"You may think this is all about an interview. That's where you're wrong. One interview leads to a book deal. That book deal leads to movie rights. We're talking college, paid for. A car, paid for. Money in your pocket. If it makes you feel uncomfortable, you can set up a charity in the names of your friends. What I'm talking about are choices. Choices for your future."

Hearing him speak about my experience as something to market is…strange. "I'm not ready for this."

"I understand." He reaches into his suit. "Here's my card." He gets up. "I'll be honest with you, Emily. I'm not one of those people who think things happen for a reason. I've seen too much unfairness. Senselessness. Greed. The world is a hard place. But I'm a big believer in the lemons-to-lemonade theory. You've been through something I can't imagine. You can take this horrible thing and turn it into something positive. I think you're owed that. It's the only way life makes sense." He holds his gaze for a moment and then leaves.

I look at the card. It's from a famous Hollywood talent agency.

I knew I was a story: a story to my school and to the airline. I never considered any wider interest. I never considered people would want to listen to what I had to say. I think of the first time I was ever in a limousine. It was for my grandfather's funeral. I admit I loved being in a sleek, black car behind tinted windows as the eyes of strangers rested on my mother and I, wondering who was inside.

That's how I feel now.

Wanted and interesting.

But for all the wrong reasons.

On the shore, we picked off leeches. Only a few days ago I would've been freaking out over these slimy things, little black ribbons swaying from my legs, and yet I was calm and numb. Too calm, too numb. Moving through the motions, picking them off, my hands glided across the stubble growing on my legs. How fast we devolve, I thought.

Before today, we'd had hope. We could think of home as a real thing, a certainty. Being in the jungle was just what Nico had said: an adventure, an interruption. No longer. A shift had occurred, and our spirits were buried under a blanket of despair.

It reminded me of the time I tried my mother's Ativan. I had opened my mother's orange-hued medicinal bottle and popped two of the small pills. I thought I'd feel high, slightly giggly, something to erase my insecurity, how I didn't fit in, might never fit in. Sure enough, life's edges were sanded smooth, and I saw the drug's appeal with its I-could-care-less effect until my thinking grew muddy, my energy sagged, and all I wanted was sleep.

That's all I wanted now: to sleep, give up and fade away.

Someone whispered, "It's over." It was Viv.

Of all of us, Molly had a reason to keep going—her unborn baby. She, too, sat amongst us, inert. She looked at us and said, "I used to wear small shoes when I was younger."

We looked at her, curious about this weird non sequitur.

"I kept thinking," Molly continued, "if I wore these tiny shoes, my body would stop growing. I would stop getting fat. I would become normal. I wore them all through elementary school and my feet hurt." She gazed at us, trying to make something clear. "I wasn't mean. I was in pain."

Silence descended on us.

Molly added, "I just wanted someone to know. In case…something happened. I never wanted to be Mean Molly. I wanted to be something else."

After sharing her secret and to make her feel less alone, I said, "I'm jealous of you all. Your money."

Derek sat next to me and he got the drift. He said, "I'm a virgin."

Nico looked at me and I realized my mistake in talking at all.

Anxiety filled my body. I tried to telepathically say *no, no, no*.

He said, "I don't have any regrets."

And just like that, I was relieved. Thank God for small favors.

Viv said, "I fought with my mom before I left for the airport. I don't remember my last words, but they weren't nice. They weren't I love you. I don't even remember what we were arguing about. Something about me having to call her every night." She reached into her empty pocket and let out a mournful laugh. "I'm so stupid. That's where I usually keep my cellphone." She held back her tears. "I wanted to leave her a message. To tell her…I'm sorry."

I reached out and touched her leg. "You'll tell her yourself when you get back. When we get back."

"What if I don't? What if none of us do?"

"One of us will," I said. "And we'll tell her."

Molly said, "Can someone tell my parents, too?"

I said, "I think that goes for everybody, right?" Everyone silently nodded.

Molly said, "Can we promise that whoever makes it out…they won't let people forget?"

Another nod from the group. We were quiet a long time, our pact confirming our fears as we wrestled with our memories—things done and things not; regrets; an endless litany of coulda-woulda-shouldas.

This might be the last place I'd ever see. It was too sad to comprehend.

Some feelings can only be described as a lack of feeling. That's how we were. Our souls were punctured and deflating.

Viv laughed to mask her tears, her sorrow hiding her anger. "This can't be...I had things I was going to do."

Nico cocked his head. "What things, Viv? Tell us, what grand things were you going to do?"

Viv looked at him as if he'd slapped her. "Why are you being so mean?"

"I never heard what you were going to accomplish. I only heard about shopping, video games, or what dumb show was on Bravo. So tell us. Why does the world care about Vivian Liu?"

"The world cares because *I* was in it. I was a good person. I worked hard. I deserved it."

"I think if the jungle has taught us anything," Nico scoffed, "it's that nature doesn't give a shit."

"The world isn't the jungle."

"That's where you're wrong."

Viv's upper lip started to tremble. "You're my boyfriend. You're supposed to be nice to me. To be my hero."

"You don't get it, do you?"

Oh God, no.

"No, I don't. You've been acting weird ever since the crash—"

"Considering the circumstances, I've been acting fairly normal. And what I can't take anymore is your poor-me attitude." He took a mocking tone. "'I had things I was going to do.' Didn't we all? Or is this just an episode of The Viv Show where everything works out at the end? I don't think Ryan was ever the dead weight here. It was *you*."

Derek placed his hand near his face, taking in the show with not-so-hidden glee.

The words crushed Viv and she grew quiet. "Do you love me?"

I could see the word on Nico's lips, his tongue pressing against the top of his mouth, and I knew what he would say. I couldn't let him. "He does, Viv. He does."

Nico squinted, taking my challenge. "What would it take for you *not* to love me, Viv?"

"I'd always love you."

I couldn't stop it, there was nothing to do. I watched, paralyzed, my own guilt eating me from within.

"No matter what?" Nico said.

"Nico, why are you doing this?" I said.

"Because if we're going to die, I want to say how I feel. Because I can't stand the hypocrisy." Nico turned to me. "You, acting like you're Viv's best friend."

Viv caught my eyes. "What's he talking about?"

"Nothing. He's just being a dick."

My heart raced and I had to urge to run. To be anywhere but here.

Nico said, "Because I slept with Emily."

The air went quiet or maybe that was my imagination. I didn't hear anything except my breath. Across from me, Derek was clapping, his mouth open in a gaping laugh. Molly smirked, taking pleasure that the world had meted out punishment for everyone. Nico got up and stretched, as if the truth had set him free, and I felt Viv's eyes on me. I didn't dare look up.

CHAPTER TWENTY

I remember asking Johannes as I lay next to him in bed, "Why do you write?"

"What do you mean?"

"I mean, is it like gardening? Something you do? Otherwise, why do it? It's not like anyone reads it." His eyes fell, and I realized I'd hurt him. "I didn't mean it like that. You know I think you're talented. It's why I'm here. 'Cause it's not your good looks."

He smiled at my joke. "I wish I knew. Certainly not for the money. Sometimes it's a blessing. Sometimes, a curse." He considered. "I think it's a way to make sense of the senseless. To reorder chaos. Real answer?"

I nodded.

"To bed hot chicks."

I smacked him in the arm. "Writers don't have groupies."

"Says who?" He nodded towards me.

"I am <u>not</u> a groupie."

"Keep telling yourself that and it might come true."

As I write this sitting in my hospital room, tapping on a keyboard, I think of what he said. Not about me being a writer groupie, that's absurd. But if you keep telling yourself something, by pure repetition words might manifest into reality. Things could come true. That could happen, right?

The day of the trip, I packed my bags, grabbed my passport and arranged a ride with Viv. I waited until my mom had left for work, which made carrying my bags out the door much less risky. The last thing I did was scribble a note to my mother: *I went to South America. Don't be mad. I'll be back in ten days.*

I thought of all her notes I'd read over the years. Or worse, when there were no notes at all.

Was I a terrible daughter? Or a renaissance woman who would not be stopped?

At the airport, I counted down the minutes until we boarded. At any time, I expected a public announcement to ring through the airport: "Ms. Emily Duran, please report to security. Ms. Emily Duran, please report to security." In doing so, I would find my mother seething. And though she wasn't the grounding type (ignoring me was her pleasure), she could send me to one of those military-style boarding schools for my senior year.

Even as I handed the airline representative my boarding pass, I expected him to stop and pull me off to the side. Walking through the tunnel-like passage to the plane was no better: I felt beads of sweat forming on my brow.

Only when I sat on the plane next to an exit row over the wing did I relax about one thing and grow anxious about another. I had made my escape and now I was trapped in a metal tube that would fly thousands of feet in the air in a contraption made by humans. I made mistakes *daily*. I imagined the hundreds of people responsible for the plane's creation and maintenance, the intricate wiring and design and how one mistake could cascade, bringing this bucket of bolts crashing to the ground.

They were not comforting thoughts.

At that moment, I was actually jealous of the six seniors who had smuggled alcohol into prom. They'd been caught by the reeking scent on their breath, helped in no part by one of their dates who puked up what looked like awful modern art. As seniors, the school couldn't stop them from graduating, so their only recourse was to ban them from taking the end-of-year trip. Six empty seats dotted the aircraft. (The flight would later take on mythical status as the number of students who "almost took the trip" soared.)

If I had ever been caught in my own Hitchcockian dolly-zoom, this was it. I fought the urge to get off the plane then and there. Luckily, I'd pawned a couple of my mother's Ativan and after scrounging in my cross-body bag I popped one. In that moment, I felt a kinship with my mother and understood how overwhelming life could be. These pills were like mental Band-Aids. Every minute that passed brought relief as calm infused my body. I made sure to keep my bag close in case I needed any more.

Once all the students were settled, Johannes found our row and moved awkwardly past Viv. She mouthed to me, still having no idea of my relationship, *nice butt*.

"Hi, Mr. DeKoning," I said, suppressing a smile.

"Hi, Ms. Liu. Ms. Duran." He sat in the middle, totally professional, totally at ease, and very debonair with two women flanking him.

Minutes later, the engines revved, the jet rolled down the tarmac, and we were floating up and into the air, and I remembered Johannes' take on flying and thought: William Shakespeare would love this, indeed.

In the jungle, Viv sat across from me. Everyone else had gotten up. In a matter of seconds, she went from being my best friend to my former best friend. I wanted her to lash out, scream and yell, call me names, push me into the dirt, anything to give voice to her betrayal. And yet nothing she could do would make me feel worse or more punished than I felt already. I thought of all the times I'd heard her laugh, her joyful giggle, and I knew I would never hear it again. Not with me, at least. Relationships took so long to build, and yet all it took was one loose thread to unravel everything.

I hated myself. There were no words, just a hole. A deep, never-ending hole and me falling into it.

Viv remained quiet, and I didn't meet her face.

"Viv," I said, "It's not what you think. It happened *once*. It happened before you were dating. We were just hanging out and...." I trailed off. "It's no excuse. I should've told you. I *meant* to tell you. That's why I never wanted to hang out with you guys. It was too awkward and I felt like I was keeping a secret, and the more I kept it inside, the bigger it got. The more time went on, the more I thought: don't ruin your friendship, no one has to know, no one will ever know."

But I always knew. It's the reason I went to prom with Derek. I was paying back a debt to the universe, balancing out the scales. Putting out good karma to alleviate the bad. I don't think it mattered in the end.

"I feel terrible, Viv, but…I'm also relieved. Even if I'm not your friend anymore, I'm glad you know."

I waited for Viv to reply and realized I never said I was sorry. I met her eyes to tell her and the look on her face stopped me. I was expecting anger or tears, maybe shock, but what was scarier was her calmness. Her perma-smile was gone, replaced with the face of a mannequin, cold and empty.

"I'm sorry," I sputtered. "I wish I could take it back. I wish I could take it all back."

I began crying and the tears were warm on my face. I'd been trying to stay strong these past few days, and I let it out. This trip had ruined everything. I had ruined everything.

My body heaved, and I felt so alone. My best friend was gone. We were lost. I was lost.

Then I felt Viv's body around mine, her arms around me. For a split second, I thought she might be getting into position to strangle me. Instead, she hugged me. Viv was *hugging* me, which only made me feel worse.

"Em," she said. "It doesn't matter."

"Yes, it does."

"Nothing matters. We'll pretend it never happened."

"But it did."

She released her hug and looked me right in the eye. "Nothing happened, Emily. Nothing ever happened." Viv stood up and walked away.

The rest of the group lingered on the outskirts, pretending not to watch. Whatever fireworks they expected, they didn't get. I wanted to shout *show's over!* Actually, I wanted to go back in time to have never gotten on that plane, to have never gone to that party. So many things, so many regrets.

Nico stood away from the group, looking off into the distance.

I pressed up from the mud and approached him. I wanted to slap him. "Why did you do that?"

"I don't expect you to understand, Em. There was my life before the crash, and then there's whatever it'll be after. I don't have a past anymore. Only this. And I want to move forward."

"It's the worst thing you could've done."

"You're one to talk."

What was done was done, yet I didn't want the crash to take everything from us. I needed us to come out of this experience stronger, not weaker.

"What about prom? Didn't you two, you know?"

"We did. But you know who I was thinking about the whole time?" He found my eyes. "The only reason I hung out with her was to be close to you. There, I said it. I thought, maybe over time, you'd see me. Like you did that night."

I almost laughed. Here was Nico, a guy I used to like in another life, a guy I was too shy to talk to, only to end up with him and to find out he liked me, too. The universe gave me everything I ever wanted, just at the wrong time.

I said, "It's never going to happen, Nico."

His face fell. I think he always held out hope. Without hope, he grew cold. "I see," he said. "I guess I have my answer."

"I think you do."

"Then I know what I need to do."

"What does that even mean?"

"It means I'm done."

At least there was closure. I could move on. Viv could move on. Nico could move on. As I watched him walk away, I died a little inside.

After that, Viv ignored Nico. She didn't even glance at him. It was like he didn't exist. She wasn't much better with me. At night, Nico slept next to Derek and Viv slept next to Molly. I slept alone. As exhausted and sore as I was, my guilty conscience conspired to keep me awake.

Could I repair my relationship? Was it possible?

Help me, I implored silently.

I thought I had known loneliness. It was nothing compared to now. I was banished. An outcast.

I watched as everyone's breathing slowed and one by one, they fell asleep. I must have followed shortly thereafter for suddenly it was morning, bringing with it the same screeches and whirring insects, the mud on our faces dry and cracked. I took a breath of air, sat up and stretched. Lifting my shirt, I could see the outline of my ribcage. All the magazines I read had made that xylophone bone seem sexy and so out of reach, and now I was showing signs of it. I wasn't flattered; I was starving. I rolled my shirt back down.

Looking over the rest of us, I noticed Derek slept alone. Nico was missing. I waited, listening to see if he was in the wall of green, but the constant noise made it difficult. Minutes passed. A bathroom break wouldn't have taken that long. I held off waking everyone up, as I didn't think the group could handle any more drama.

So I waited.

He's trying to gather some mushrooms, that's all.

The sun continued to rise.

I tried to rationalize: *he's off doing…doing what? What excuse could there be?*

Something was wrong.

"Guys! Guys!" I got up and shook them awake. They looked at me, eyes glazed with sleep. "Nico's gone."

Viv didn't ask a single question.

Derek said, "How long?"

"I don't know. Fifteen, twenty minutes?"

Derek rose and took in the empty space next to his bed. He stood up, trying to see movement in the distance. He cupped his mouth and yelled, "Ni-co! Ni-co!"

By now all of us were up, Molly, too, searching our campsite and the outskirts.

I said, "I don't see any blood. Or signs of his clothes." That had to be a good sign, right?

Molly said, "Where would he have gone?"

Derek said, "Can't be far. There's nothing out there."

We screamed his name, waiting for a reply.

Nothing.

"Guys." We turned. It was Viv.

"The bag. The bag with the food. It's gone."

CHAPTER TWENTY-ONE

My cross-body bag filled with mushrooms was gone. So was Nico. He must've stolen the food during the night and left. That's what he meant when he said he knew what he had to do. I shouldn't have been surprised—anyone who would break up with his girlfriend under these circumstances was selfish beyond repair. But I was. Desperation either brought people together or it ripped them apart. Nico had made his choice.

Anger and frustration flashed across our faces. I could feel us contract from each other; no one was to be trusted. If Nico had taken the food and run off, then anyone was capable of anything.

Viv shook her head. "Why? Why did he do it? Where does he think he's going to go?"

Derek said, "I don't know what he's thinking. He doesn't know the first thing about survival."

I didn't think he was thinking at all. He was running; away from us; away from me. In anger or disgrace, I didn't know. Maybe he realized what a huge mistake he'd made and had a delayed reaction. Rather than stay, he left. He and his foolish pride.

Molly said, "I told you I didn't steal the food before. See?"

It didn't prove anything. Molly could've taken the food the first time. Hell, anyone could have. But I didn't want to argue.

Derek spotted something on the ground. He walked from the wall of green. "He didn't go into the jungle." Muddy footprints led to the river's edge. "He's walking along the river."

"How far is he?"

"He's got a good head start, that's for sure." Derek grabbed his hatchet and walked off.

Viv said, "You're going after him?"

Derek turned. "I'm going after our food."

We scampered after Derek as he followed the footprints, and as he said, they led to the water's edge. The river was wide, the current strong. Nico wasn't going to swim and he wasn't going to head back to the crash site. That left only one direction and we took it. After a few paces, Derek stooped over. He came back with the remnants of a mushroom stem. The insult was made even greater by Nico's waste.

Viv asked, "What are you going to do when you find him?"

Derek turned the hatchet in his hands. "I don't know. I honestly don't know."

Nico must've gotten quite a head start, for it was at least a couple of hours before we spotted him hedging close to the water's edge. He was still a few football fields out. I wondered what was the point of either us following, or him running. We were all heading in the same direction, bound to end up in the same place. The only thing certain was awkwardness when we all met again.

But seeing him increased the group's determination and our tempo increased.

"Nico," I shouted, and he turned around.

Almost simultaneously, Derek hissed, "Why did you do that? Now he knows we're here."

"It's not like we were going to sneak up on him."

Nico saw us, and maybe we seemed like a mob chasing after Frankenstein's monster, Derek's hatchet reflecting the sun, and he bolted off.

"Nico! Don't! We're not going to hurt you! We just want the food!" If he heard my cries, he didn't stop. He started running over the uneven terrain. Like dogs chasing prey, the group only seemed more intent on catching him. I overheard Molly telling Derek, "....stole our food. Can't let him get away with it." We'd become a posse and Nico was the outlaw. I almost wished he'd get away. Almost.

We continued this slow-speed chase for most of the day, the sun beating down, him ahead, us behind, sometimes gaining, sometimes lagging, this stalemate of walking, and for what? Mushrooms? Or vengeance?

"Guys," I said. "Forget him. Let's just go foraging. We need food." The sticky humid air was sapping my strength.

"We'll get food, all right," Derek said, his face glistening with sweat. "We'll get food."

"I meant now."

Derek didn't break his stride. "If we let Nico get away with it, then everyone knows they can do the same thing."

There were so many things wrong with that statement. "What are you talking about? No one's going to do it again."

"That's what we thought the first time."

I wanted to tell him I thought *he* had stolen the food the first time. I held my tongue. The accusation would only sow more distrust. I said, "I thought we just wanted his food."

"Plan changed." Clearly, the journey had made him angry, every step bringing into focus our lack of food, fueling our mission, even though we always intended to go this direction.

"I'm not wasting my energy," I said, "chasing down one of our friends— to what? Beat him up? How will that help?"

"He's not our friend. Not anymore."

"Just let him go."

"You go," Derek spat. "If you want."

I looked from face to face and no one took my side. Not even Viv.

Now I knew how Derek felt right after the crash when we landed on shore and he wanted to turn toward the crash site, but no one would go with him. I didn't want to be alone. I *couldn't* be alone. I could survive with the group.

Without it, I was nothing. Hating my weakness, I trudged along with them.

Our group mentality gave us the strength and purpose in spite of our hunger. Ahead, Nico stumbled, and I could sense his tiredness, his weakening resolve. I doubted he would try to hide: there were too many stinging insects and unknowns lurking under every leaf. We gained, minute-by-minute, while he slowed. As he saw us, he gave a last spurt of energy and ran.

"Viv," I said. "Are you gonna let this happen?"

"What do you want me to do?"

"Tell Derek to stop. He'll listen to you."

Viv considered, seconds passing. She said quietly, "Nico stole our food."

I was too stunned to move. Viv's damsel-in-distress was gone and it its place was someone I didn't recognize. I watched as Molly and Viv walked ahead of me. I wondered if we were worth saving at all.

"Nico!" Derek yelled, his lean body hopping over stumps and exposed tree roots like a forest creature. "Give us our food! You stole our food!"

Throw the bag, I mentally implored. Just throw the bag and run.

Nico disappeared behind a bend of trees. Derek quickly caught up and followed. They couldn't be more than a few yards apart by now. Behind the wall of green, I heard a long scream and then it abruptly stopped. The silence terrified me.

Molly and Viv rushed into the jungle and out of view.

More silence.

I was alone as I ran on the river's edge, my mind racing, imagining scenarios, each one worse than the next, and then I turned into the overgrowth.

Ahead of me, Viv, Derek, and Molly stood on the lip of a rock crevice. Nico was nowhere in sight.

No, please, no....

Derek told me, his arm outstretched like a traffic cop, "Watch your step."

I carefully approached the lip, wary of slipping, and saw it was the edge of a small cliff. It reminded me of a miniature Grand Canyon. I held on to a nearby tree branch. I didn't want to see, but I had to. I had to know.

About three stories below, Nico's body lay at the bottom, his legs splayed at an impossible angle. It was far enough down that he'd had time to think, time to realize what was happening. The scream had been his.

I cupped my hands to my face and my breath left me. No one said anything. Out in the open, wind whipped against us.

"What happened?"

Derek said, "I ran after him. He didn't see the cliff until it was too late. He couldn't stop...."

A thought came unbidden: Did Nico fall? Or was he pushed?

Derek saw something in my face, a question on my lips. "I'm not a murderer, Em."

No one had seen anything. We had to believe him on faith. But if Derek had poisoned Ryan....

Nico was pushed, Nico was pushed.

Molly, unsure, stepped back from the edge.

Yet, there was nothing to be done. Nothing to prove. We would keep our secrets and survive. Survival trumped all.

I lied. "I believe you."

Viv stayed looking over at Nico, her face devoid of expression.

I had the weirdest thought she would jump after him, falling into death like a Romeo and Juliet story playing itself out in the wild. I stepped to her. "Viv?"

When she met my eyes, I knew I was wrong. I sensed she wanted to push *me*. My body tensed, but I stayed right there as if daring Fate. If my best friend was going to kill me, then maybe this is the penance I needed, the penance I deserved.

"He's still breathing," she said, as though reciting a fact in class.

Once again I looked over the side, rooting my feet as firmly as I could into the ground.

Below me, amid the silence, Nico's chest swelled in and out.

"He's alive," I said.

I scanned the jungle floor and saw a way down. It wasn't a path—nothing near a trodden path—but it was traversable if I was careful. If I was *very* careful.

I asked Viv, "Did you want to say goodbye?"

"He said goodbye to me, remember?"

How fast love turns to hate.

I moved to the small opening leading downward and held onto a branch. Walking backwards, I made sure my foot was on steady ground before shifting my weight to the next foot. The angle was steep, but luckily not a straight drop. I grasped the tree roots like gnarled ropes, one foot at a time, careful not to slip, and it reminded me of my road trips to Joshua Tree National Park and climbing rock formations.

No one followed. They watched me from the lip as I snaked my way further and further down, tiny avalanches of dirt matching my descent. I never liked heights. My body was anxious at being so far out of my comfort zone. I concentrated on my breath. In and out, steadying my rhythm.

More roots, more steps.

The closer I got to the bottom, I realized Nico hadn't just fallen; he'd tumbled, hitting branches that were now bent, and jagged rock in his split-second but eternal drop.

I finally stepped on the bottom.

Up close, Nico's body was in way worse shape than he seemed from afar. There was no way he would walk. No way he would move. I was surprised he'd even survived. Aside from his original injuries from the crash, the bruises and cuts and scrapes, his body was littered with new wounds, the bones of his legs broken like a shattered set of Jenga blocks. Pain must've overwhelmed him into unconsciousness. Tangled among his limbs was my cross-body bag.

Lifting the flap, it was empty. Our foot chase had been for nothing. How long had the mushrooms been gone? It didn't matter. These were facts: Nico was severely injured. There was no way I could carry him on a bamboo stretcher. And I doubted anyone in the group would volunteer to share the load.

Nico would die here, that was certain.

But he was alive now.

Derek yelled from above, his voice echoing down, "IS THERE FOOD?"

That was his first question. Not *Is he all right?* Not *What do we do?* Not *Can we save him?*

I looked at the empty bag, considering the ramifications of my answer. "Yes. There's some left."

"GOOD."

If I had told him there wasn't any food, I feared they'd leave immediately, and maybe even leave me. If I had food, I was valuable. I was worth waiting for.

As if reading my thoughts, Derek called down: "WHAT ARE YOU WAITING FOR?"

Then Nico gasped. His eyes were open, his head lying on the ground as if it were detached, like a robotic piece left over from a useless body. Nothing else moved, just the muscles around his lips and eyes.

"I'm sorry," he whispered. Blood trickled from his mouth.

"It's okay," I said dumbly, not knowing what else to say.

"Can you…reach into my pocket? I can't move my fingers." He motioned with his eyes. "Give me the rest of what's in there."

I rummaged through his pocket, wondering if I was causing him more pain. If so, he didn't wince. I drew out the plastic baggie. It was empty. There weren't even seeds or tiny bits of grass-like pieces. "I'm sorry, Nico," and I showed him the baggie.

He coughed and spit out more blood. He shut his eyes and all was still. I thought he had died. After a moment, his lips moved. "I'm not gonna make it, am I?"

Did he want honesty? What else was there?

"Rest," I said. "You've come a long way."

Nico glanced at his broken watch and tried to joke. "Some things can't be fixed, can they?" He laughed and it morphed into a cry. He softly sang, the lyrics jumbled and nonsensical.

"WHAT ARE YOU DOING DOWN THERE?" Derek's voice rattled the tranquility. I wanted to tell him to shut up. No matter Nico's "crime," he deserved a peaceful death.

Nico's song became more of a hum, and then he stopped. He was winded. "Can you stay here with me…?"

I didn't know how long it would be—minutes, an hour? I didn't think

Derek and the group would wait that long. I hated weighing Nico's needs against my own, computing my survival against his death.

Nico said, "I don't want the animals...."

Come nightfall, if not sooner, they would rip him apart. I wanted to protect him. But I couldn't. I knew Derek was right and I cursed his logic as his voice pinballed in my head: *this is survival.*

I decided to wait a little bit and hope he would pass. It couldn't be too much longer.

"EMILY! WHAT ARE YOU DOING?"

Nico opened his eyes. "Go."

Seconds passed, each one an entire universe. His last words to me were "The sun feels nice."

I started back up the path, and going up was much harder. Step by step, I rose from the depths, climbing to Molly, Viv, and Derek, leaving death behind and moving to life. My tears blurred my vision and I had to wipe them away. I had to steel myself to climb back up. I promised myself I would cry oceans of tears, but right now I couldn't. I climbed and I rose. I decided not to look back. I wanted to remember Nico alive. I wanted to remember him as the man who had loved me. Or maybe I didn't want the image of his dying—dying alone because he'd been chased—burned into my mind.

CHAPTER TWENTY-TWO

In the hospital, I wake to the sounds of faint clicking. I've been sleeping a lot and it's less from exhaustion and more from depression. Dreaming is my escape, my drug. There's too much pressure to live up to the preciousness of life when compared to the absence of everyone else's. It's a burden I don't want and never asked for, as though all the deeds and things they would've accomplished now belong to me. I have to make up for their loss. I will never cure cancer; I will never change the world; I will barely be remembered after my own death. So how can I measure up?

Across from me my mother sits on a chair, laptop open, and she's reading and scrolling down, her fingers tapping with a click, click, click.

Reading my journal.

"Mom."

She looks up, and I understand the cliché of a deer in headlights. "I'm sorry," she says. "I didn't know it was private."

"It is."

She still doesn't shut it. "But you were so brave."

"Mom, please turn it off."

"I must've done something right, then, to raise you like that."

She must've read the parts I wrote about *her*. "It's just my way of getting things down. Explaining things. Like the counselor said."

"Well, it's very good."

"I don't care if it's good." It occurs to me this isn't the first time she's been reading. She's probably been sneaking peeks every time I fall asleep. "You called that agent guy, didn't you?"

She looks at the window with its closed blinds as if picturing the view outside. "I just thought…on some level, I knew what you had gone through, but to *read* it…I'm sorry you had to experience that. You like to think you can protect your kid, not that I was a great parent…." I don't argue with her. "But you hope. And I thought—people have to know." There's steeliness in her voice. "People have to know my daughter didn't suffer for nothing." She pauses and looks at me. "Are you mad?"

"I wish you would've asked me first."

"I meant to."

The things *I meant to*, as well. Like mother, like daughter.

"I wish you would've told me," she says, "about your relationship."

"With my teacher? Yeah, that would've gone over real well."

"I think you forget I know what it's like to be in love. To love the wrong man." She smiles. "Or men." When I don't fill in the empty silence, she asks, "Did you love him?"

"I think so."

"Did he love you?"

I don't answer.

"He seemed like…an interesting man."

"Is that your way of calling him a pervert?"

"I didn't mean it like that." She sighs. "I don't want to fight with you, Em. I want to be your friend."

I want to say: *And I want a mother.* "It's easy to say now."

"I know." She finally closes the laptop and places it on my bed.

We sit in silence. I say, "I'm sorry I left the note for you." I'm sorry for a lot of things. Guilt eats at me like a withering disease and I think of all the pain and worry I've caused. My life is filled with so many bad decisions and there's no way to erase them.

"At least," my mother says, "something good came from that trip. Us talking. Really talking."

I'm 17, soon to be 18, and then out of the house, probably forever. Why couldn't we have talked before? Why did it take a tragedy to say how we feel?

She fidgets with her fingers, probably craving a cigarette. "You made me think about things. Things that need changing. Things I've been ignoring for a long time. What you went through, what you did to survive…I can't let you down anymore."

She kisses my forehead. "I'm proud of you, Emily. I'm sorry I never told you that. Or how beautiful you are. I'm proud you're my daughter."

I can see tears welling in her eyes, and she excuses herself before she loses control.

When I reached the top of the cliff, Derek grasped my hand and helped heave me up. Once safe, I moved away from the ledge. He took my cross-body bag, looked inside, and had the look of someone who has smelled something bad.

"I thought you said there was some left."

"I know, but when I looked, they were covered in blood." The lie slid easily off my lips. "We couldn't eat bloody mushrooms."

"We could've washed them off. It's not like Nico had AIDS."

"Sorry, I wasn't thinking."

He rummaged through the bag. "I don't see any blood in here. No stains. There's nothing wet."

"Do you think I'm lying?"

He eyed me suspiciously. "I know you, Emily. I know you're not telling me something. And I want to know why."

"I told you."

"Turn out your pockets."

"What?"

"You heard me," he said.

"I didn't take any mushrooms, Derek." He stood in front me, arms crossed, waiting. I could've thrown a fit, but I was too tired, and it was easier to acquiesce. "Fine." My pockets were empty. "Satisfied?"

"You could've eaten them. No one would've seen you."

"You're right. I could've eaten them. But I didn't." To prove my point, I opened my mouth to let him inspect. He didn't.

"Then why'd you lie?"

I figured the truth was better than him thinking I'd eaten food meant for the group. "I wanted you to wait for me."

He cocked his head like a confused dog. "You think we would've *left* you down there? That I would've left you?" His confusion turned to disgust. "Who do you think we are? I thought we were friends."

"We are."

He lifted the empty cross-body bag and threw it back at me. "Sure feels like it."

"Derek...."

"Never mind." He walked off, joining Molly and Viv.

As we made our way back to the river's edge, I thought of Ryan and Nico. Two bodies never to be seen again, lost to the jungle, bones scattered. I hated the jungle and yet I didn't say it aloud. Nico had and he was dead. I knew it was irrational, but it seemed that to criticize the jungle out loud was to welcome a curse. As if the jungle would hear and focus all of its efforts so that I would never leave its grip ever again.

It was Molly who asked me, "What did he say?"

It took me a moment to realize she meant Nico. I turned to Viv, and she wasn't interested; her legs were like the pendulum of a clock, always moving.

His last words belonged to me. I wouldn't share them. "He didn't say anything."

"You were down there long enough."

"You could've come with."

Molly motioned towards her belly. "I couldn't risk it."

I kept forgetting Molly was pregnant. I didn't know any pregnant people, and I didn't know what their symptoms were. I laughed—*symptoms*, as if being pregnant was a condition or a disease. At least in the midst of all this death, there was something comforting to know there was life among us, too. A life that wouldn't know this horror. A life I hoped that would be born someplace far from here.

"Have you thought of any names?" I asked.

"I don't know." After a few moments, she said, "Maybe 'John' if he was a boy. After his dad. I haven't thought if it's a girl. Something scarier about a girl, you know? Guys always love their mothers, but it's the daughters who hate their moms."

True enough, I thought.

"Why don't you call her Molly, Jr. Guys do it. Why can't women?"

"Or maybe MJ," she said. "Short for Molly, Jr."

"MJ could stand for Molly-John."

"That's perfect!"

Weirdly enough, I was glad to help. My little contribution to this unborn baby could very well last its entire life.

We kept walking, destined to walk downriver, towards the river, towards a hypothetical village, and I thought life was the same way. We chose a direction, walk that path, and hope for the best. Hope didn't come easy. It had to be continuously created and called upon or it would disappear as soon as something else took its place—an itch, thought, thirst, hunger. It was Hope versus Everything Else.

Viv walked in front of me. She seemed beyond hope.

"Viv," I said. "Are you okay?" I mentally chastised myself for asking such a stupid question. "You haven't said anything since…."

"I'm okay, Emily." She said it with such politeness, but she seemed dead behind the eyes.

"I don't think you are, Viv."

"Did I ever tell you I spent Nico's birthday with his family?" Her voice was flat. There was no joy, no inflection. "There were balloons and cake, and wine. His father let us have some if we didn't drive. Later, Nico's dad inhaled a balloon full of helium. With his squeaky voice he imitated the Munchkins, singing 'I'm a part of the Lollipop Guild' and he ended with Tiny Tim's 'God Bless Us Everyone.' I loved his family. They were so different than my own. I thought I'd be a part of them forever."

"That's sweet, Viv. I know they loved you."

"Nico didn't. That's all that matters, isn't it?" I was about to speak when she cut me off. "Don't deny it. I know. I never made him laugh. Not like you did. He thought you were clever. I was a fool to believe he ever cared."

"I care, Viv."

"I know, Emily. You're my best friend." It felt worse to hear her say it and even worse that it was devoid of emotion. It was as if she were repeating a fact, trying to convince herself. She gave a forced smile, walked away and caught up to Derek. It seemed as if they were pairing off, leaving Molly and me behind.

I'm just being paranoid, I thought.

Turns out I wasn't paranoid enough.

CHAPTER TWENTY-THREE

I used to watch the occasional episode of *Survivor* and it always amazed me at how quickly the contestants went from looking healthy to skin-and-bones. After only a few days in the jungle, we were no different. Viv couldn't afford to lose any more weight. She looked coltish, hipbones protruding, verging on the skeletal. We were all on the "jungle diet," but she looked the worst for wear.

Molly trudged with me, and I thought it best to try and make peace.

"I liked your poem," I said.

"You read it?"

I nodded. "I saw it in class." I caught myself about to say his first name. "Mr. DeKoning said you were talented."

She seemed surprised. "He did?"

"He never told you that?"

"No," Molly said.

"I thought he would've." We passed underneath some low hanging trees. I don't know why I asked; I guess I was curious how he treated her. "Did you guys ever go out or did you just spend time at his apartment?"

"I don't really want to talk about him, if that's all right."

"Sure," I said.

But Molly didn't continue with any conversation. That left me with pretty much no one to talk to.

As the day unfolded, we ate mushrooms and grubs, and sometimes drank water that dripped from vines. Viv, Molly, and I retreated into our own little worlds while Derek seemed to expand. The jungle was becoming his playground. He got excited at his discoveries, like the vines with water or identifying the Brazilian wandering spider. Somewhere along the way he'd morphed into a giddy, walking Bill Nye The Science Guy. One of us was happy, at least.

Time had become meaningless and at some point during the day we turned away from the river. There was no way to walk on the edge, so we entered the jungle and kept our direction. Unless my eyes were playing tricks on me, it seemed brighter up ahead. That could mean only one thing: we were approaching some kind of open space, and I wondered if we would soon emerge into a village.

A village, a village, a village.

I pulled back a branch, the lazy sunlight on the other side like some kind of angelical apparition, and we stepped out of the jungle and into what was most definitely *not* a village. How foolish of me to think there would be salvation here. Instead of a field with huts and cows and people, it was a muddy, wet dirt road about as wide as a four-lane highway, and it ran as far as the eye could see, disappearing into the horizon. Beneath us, the dirt was reddish, and it was riddled with muddy holes. Scattered rocks littered the area. Portions were flooded over with brown water where mosquitoes danced on their surface. It seemed completely impassable by vehicle. There was off-roading, and then there was this, a road in name only.

A road usually meant civilization. Transportation. People. But this looked long abandoned. That made it even more depressing, as if it were a road to nowhere.

Molly asked, "Is this what they mean by deforestation and clear-cutting?" I pictured a giant barber coming through and giving the area a buzz cut. The jungle was thick on either side, but as for the road itself there wasn't a single tree.

Viv surprised us all when she said, "I think it's the Trans Amazon

Highway." As if reciting from memory, she explained the Trans Amazon Highway was a project Brazil initiated in the 1970s. A kind of Panama Canal that would cross the entire Amazon, except over land. But the project went bust. She forgot why. After she spoke, she fell back into her detached silent state.

The land reminded me of us. Of what we used to be: vibrant with high hopes, and then depleted and left behind.

"Well," Derek said, "it ain't the Yellow Brick Road, but it's something."

"Yeah," I replied. "It's something all right."

As disappointed as I was to not find a village, I was happy to get a change of scenery. No more green and its numerous variations. No more claustrophobia from a canopy above. No more snakes, tarantulas or surprises lurking around every tree stump. If I tried really hard, I could picture us walking on some backwoods country road.

My mind drifted. *If I make it back, I'm not sure I want to go back to school. If I make it back, maybe I'll just get my GED.*

Then I caught myself.

If I make it back.

If, not when.

That wasn't positive thinking. I didn't know when the shift occurred, but it had to stop. It had to stop now. If I was drifting, I could only imagine the state Viv was in.

I forced conversation. I forced normality.

"Viv, what's your favorite video game?"

She looked at me as if she hadn't heard me correctly.

"Seriously," I added.

"I don't like video games. Not anymore."

"But you used to love them."

"I used to love a lot of things, Em."

She turned and went back to her thousand-yard-stare. I couldn't let her drift away.

"C'mon, there's gotta be at least one. *BioShock*. Maybe *Call of Duty*?"

"I think of all the time, all those hours I spent playing, it's like a whole part of my life was wasted. Time I won't get back."

"What about all the turd-trucks out there? The frig-balls? All the people you made fun of? You laughed about those things. You had fun." I wanted to tell her how much I needed her to smile. For both our sakes. One smile, Viv. Please.

"It's funny," she said, her face numb. "I can't remember that now."

We finally bunked for the night. Two bamboo beds. One for Molly and me, the other for Derek and Viv. It was odd to have our beds in the middle of a road. Even though I knew we were completely remote, I couldn't help but envision an eighteen-wheeler rumbling over the hill, flattening us. The last thing I'd see before thinking *gee, we're saved* would be its bright lights blinding me.

I'd lost count of how many nights we'd slept in the jungle. I knew it was important to remember, for to stop counting was to give up hope. But there was something terrible about keeping track of misery. It felt like being held hostage, and in a way we were.

Maybe our journey really was our forty days and forty nights in the desert, as Nico had said. But if I was tempted by the Devil, I'm not so sure I'd be able to resist.

As Derek finished piecing the bed together, Viv said, "I don't think we would've survived without you."

"That's true," I said.

"Maybe I missed my calling," he joked.

He lay down on the bed, his face to the night sky. "Look at those stars. I've been in some far out places. But damn. You couldn't count 'em all if you wanted to. It's like the more you look, the more you see."

Viv reached up and grabbed into the empty air. "They look so close, it's like you could almost touch them."

"Do you see one you like?" Derek asked.

"I like 'em all."

"Pick one."

Viv searched the sky. "That one."

"Where?"

His hand followed hers up in the sky where their hands came together. "That one," she said. "The flickering one over there."

"It's yours, then."

While I thought her interaction with Derek was slightly creepy, at least she was talking like a normal person.

Molly said, "You can't just give her a star."

"There's more than enough for you. Pick one. You, too, Em. They're ours for the taking." He paused, enjoying the view. "I never look at stars in L.A. But they're always there, you know?"

I said to Derek, "Which one is yours?"

He pointed. "The one right next to Viv's."

I couldn't tell the difference. One twinkling light looked like any other. I turned my head to the side, feeling the slats of bamboo under my body and I succumbed to the dark. Derek was still stargazing and the last thing I heard before falling asleep was his voice. "It's weird," he said, "but I'm gonna miss this place."

CHAPTER TWENTY-FOUR

In the hospital, my mind keeps spinning and I stand to look out the window. I don't know what I expect to find. An answer? A sign? I open the blinds and it's dark outside. The occasional car drives past, the streetlights are on, and it's quiet. The businesses surrounding the hospital are closed, a few windows with squares of light, and I think of what people are doing up at this hour. In the sky there are only a handful of stars, dim from light pollution, so many galaxies hidden. I try to find Viv and Derek's stars.

I woke first. It was still early, given the position of the sun in the sky, and the jungle continued with its madhouse of noise. I sat up in bed, the bamboo creaking beneath me, and sensed movement nearby.

I turned and my breath stopped.

In the middle of the road was a lone jaguar. I'd seen pictures in books, one or two at the zoo, but to see one only a few yards away, in the wild, not enclosed by a cage, was both majestic and frightening. Covered in dark spots over a brown coat, it looked like an immense house cat. It was lean and muscular, an apex predator, built for speed and power. Its dark eyes gazed into mine and I sensed its presence. There was a *consciousness* behind those eyes. It stayed looking at me, and I stayed absolutely still. Around me, Viv,

Derek, and Molly slept, and I wondered if I should try to wake them.

The jaguar slunk lower and moved one large paw at a time towards me. It never looked away.

I stayed statue-still and wondered if this is how my story would end.

The animal moved closer and closer, every inch seeming like hours. My concentration never broke.

Soon it was three yards away, then two, then one.

The jaguar was almost right in front of me. So close, I could lift a hand and pet it if I tried. Its broad head was built like an anvil, and though he never opened his mouth, not to lick or pant, I knew a row of teeth lined his powerful jaws. If he wanted to attack me, there was nothing I could do. Absolutely nothing. He was the Amazon's perfect killer, and I was at the mercy of his power.

He was a stunning creature. This close, his markings didn't look like spots, but like black butterflies tattooed onto fur. He seemed to look *into* me, and I felt the same about him. How long we gazed at each other, I can't say. Seconds? Minutes?

I should've been scared; I should've wanted to scream, but I had the oddest sensation of letting go. I had been through enough. I was tired of being scared. I gazed right back, not with any intention other than *I am here, I mean you no harm.*

His ear flicked, and then as if hearing something far away, he turned and swiftly loped off. He barely made a sound. One second he was there and the next he shot away into the jungle. I reached out in the empty air right where the jaguar had been. Right there. I didn't even need to straighten my arm.

I thought of waking Viv and the rest of them to share what had happened, but I feared they wouldn't believe me. Or maybe I wanted to keep the experience for myself. I would be all right. Somehow I knew this on a deep, spiritual level. I could face anything. I had faced Death. I wondered if they would've had the same outcome.

After the encounter, I waited for the rest of them to wake at their own pace. With the sunlight hitting their faces, it wasn't long before they were up, stretching, using the bathroom, and preparing to head out.

I tried again to make conversation. "How'd you sleep?"

Viv and Molly looked at me like *how do you think?*

Derek said, "Great. Never better."

We walked down the road, and it was faster than walking through the jungle. Just a straight line, sometimes hilly, but easier than cutting through growth and watching where you stepped. Even the mosquitoes weren't as bad.

"Derek," I said, trying to keep things positive, "who was your favorite comic-book character?"

"Why?"

"I was trying to see if my guess was right."

"I'm not really into comic books, so your guess is as good as mine."

"I was gonna say Tarzan."

"Tarzan? The yodeler in the jungle? I'm disappointed, Em. Too easy." But a few steps later he added, "Now that you mention it...." He took in his surroundings. "Yeah, I can see it."

Molly asked, "Who would be your Jane?"

"You mean of you three?"

"As if we'd let you," Molly replied. "I mean of anyone."

"Who needs a Jane, anyway? Not when there's a Viv."

I saw the slightest smile from Viv. At least it was something.

In the morning haze, Derek broke into song, singing "Zip-A-Dee-Doo-Dah, Zip-A-Dee-A." I was glad to see him in such good spirits. The jungle energized him, and we needed his energy; we fed off it. So did Viv. She didn't seem to respond to me anymore, but Derek's song was infectious and she sang the chorus.

"C'mon, everyone!" he said, his hands out like a conductor. "*My oh my, what a wonderful day!*"

I didn't join in as it was a shade too close to Nico singing marching chants.

Viv said, "You should've been singing 'Follow the Yellow Brick Road.'"

"You're right, but it's not yellow."

"Muddy." Viv snapped her fingers, the most animated I'd seen her since Nico's death. "Follow the Muddy Brown Road."

"Genius! That's it!" Derek took to changing the words from 'yellow' to 'muddy' and continued to sing. No one knew the rest of the lyrics until they picked up again near "*We're off to see the Wizard, the wonderful Wizard of Oz.*" Against all reason, I joined in and somehow found myself hopping and skipping. Maybe it's exactly what we needed. Pure release, pure silliness. If a rescue plane spotted us, we would've made quite the scene.

Viv stopped singing. "Wait, that doesn't work. Who are we seeing? Not the Wizard."

Derek thought. "A native of 'Zon, like the Amazon?"

Viv sang it aloud, testing it; "We're off to see the native of 'Zon, the wonderful native of 'Zon." She shrugged, as if to say *it's not perfect, but it'll do*, and she and Derek led the song. It was horrible karaoke, but lovely to see. We all sang, and it was the first time we were all smiling. I chalked it up to loopiness, lack of sleep and total absurdity, but Derek seemed genuinely happy.

The trees were our audience and we sang and sang until we grew tired and fell into that awkward silence after laughter. For a long time it was just us and the road, our feet hitting dirt, rising and falling, the four of us never straying very far. Like the mother's warning in "Little Red Riding Hood," we stayed on the road, happy to never enter the jungle again. Though the terrain never altered, a road gave the illusion of going somewhere.

That's when we stopped in our tracks.

No one spoke. I think we all thought it was a mirage.

Ahead of us, there was a man, a man wearing a shirt and shorts. He carried a small, dead boar over his shoulder and his free hand held a wooden spear. He was about a city block away, walking.

Derek asked, his voice barely audible, "Do you see what I see?"

We were scared to believe. I was terrified. There is something indescribable at finally getting what you want but fearing to touch it. I couldn't take another disappointment. Not this close.

I shot forward, but Derek grabbed me harshly. "What if he's dangerous?"

"He's not."

"How do you know?"

"Because we've got nothing to lose." I jerked free and ran towards the man, screaming, "Hey! Over here!" Viv and Molly followed, the three of us waving our hands. I have no idea what the man thought seeing us, three hysterical girls running towards him as Derek came up the rear.

He stopped and turned, his hand tightening on the spear.

As we approached, I saw that he was short and probably native. He had teak skin, his dark hair in a basic bowl-cut, and he had a weird juxtaposition of Western clothes while going barefoot. His shirt was red and emblazoned with the Coca-Cola logo, and his pants were green board shorts. Take away his boar and spear, and he could've been a surfer.

I stopped a few feet away so as not to scare him. "English? Do you speak English?"

He shook his head and spoke in a language I didn't understand or recognize. If he looked surprised to see us, he didn't act it.

I did the clichéd American-speaking-to-a-foreigner and spoke slowly and loudly, while miming my movements. "Plane crash…we fell…from the sky….we need…help."

Seeing my hands as birdwings that fell, he nodded. He spoke calmly and seemed to understand and pointed far behind us, speaking about what I could only assume was the crash. He made a sound as if it was loud and mimed other planes in the area, even the spinning kind, which I think meant helicopters. He mimed boats, too, as he seemed to "row," and people, as he put his hand near his eyes making circles that looked like binoculars.

"People are looking for us?"

The man nodded.

Suddenly, Molly started to cry, which caused Viv to cry, and I felt tears on my face, too. We hadn't been forgotten. We'd never been forgotten.

I was overwhelmed with a mix of feelings. Joy and sadness, hope and loss, but most of all I felt *alive*. It was the happiest moment in my entire life.

"Can…you…help…us?"

He nodded and motioned for us to follow him. He pointed to the boar and rubbed his belly, and then pointed at our bellies. We were going to eat. We were going to a village. We were saved.

Thank God, we were saved.

CHAPTER TWENTY-FIVE

The hideous turbulence stopped. My heart gradually fell back to a normal rhythm. Outside, the wings stayed flat. I released my hands from the armrests and my armpits were damp with sweat. Now that the flight was level, I felt stupid. The plane had always been flying; we hadn't crashed; all was normal.

I said to Johannes, "Is it always like this?"

"No, that was definitely *not* the norm. Sorry this was your first. But wow, every time you fly after this, it's gonna be a cakewalk."

"Who says I'm flying again?"

"That'd be a shame." He leaned in and whispered. "'Cause it means we couldn't travel." He smiled and I smiled and everything was going to be okay. "To be honest, that was the worst turbulence I've ever felt. I need a drink." He pressed the Call Attendant button.

"So you get a drink and I don't?"

"Aging has its perks. Seriously, thank god there was a barf bag nearby."

"Looking on your face, I never would've known."

"I couldn't freak out if you were freaking out. I'm the one who talked you into it." He looked past me and out the window. "The only thing that keeps me sane is thinking of what it was like for people back in the day who had to cross the ocean in boats. If they hit a storm, it might be days of them slopping all over. Can you imagine that? *Days*." He shuddered and looked at the onboard map on the seatback in front of him. "Only a couple more hours. Think you can handle it?"

"Two hours is doable."

Viv unbuckled her seatbelt and said, "I'm gonna use the bathroom. Stretch my legs."

Johannes watched as she walked down the aisle. When he was sure she was gone, he reached into his carry-on bag and pulled out a small book. It was thin, more a chapbook than a paperback, and he handed it to me.

Longing For What Never Came
The Collected Poems
By Johannes DeKoning

"These are yours?" I asked. "I didn't know you wrote so many."

"It's not like I'm a Poet Laureate. It's self-published."

I ran my fingers over the spine, and then opened it up to the table of contents. There were about fifty titles listed. "What are you talking about? This is so cool. This is your work. You made this. It didn't exist before."

He was touched. "It's yours. I thought you might like it. But put it away before you-know-who comes back."

"I'd totally kiss you if I could."

"We have plenty of time." He winked.

I asked him, "Can you autograph it?"

He hesitated and then gave a *why not?* shrug. He pulled out a pen, paused and then wrote. Handing it back, he said, "It's true."

It read: *To Emily, my favorite student.*

"I better be," I joked and nudged him. "And you're my favorite teacher." I put the poetry book back in my cross-body bag, and moments later Viv sat down.

"Everybody else had the same idea," she said. "Should've seen the line. What'd I miss?"

I looked at the onboard map. "I think we flew about a quarter of an inch."

We followed the man. Molly and Viv and I hugged, our faces wet with tears. I'd never felt so happy. So relieved. So blessed. I had nothing in common with this man, not language or location, but I loved him. It was silly, but my love for him was greater than anything I'd ever experienced. All of creation radiated from him, pulsing with shockwaves of joy. He was the very center of the universe and I walked on a cloud of pure adoration.

I grabbed Derek's shoulder. "We're going home. We're going home!" I wanted to do cartwheels. Goodbye jungle, hello home! My body was about to burst; every nerve seemed to tingle, my pain receded to nothing; I felt *alive*. I shouted, "We've been rescued!"

The man looked at me, curious, but when he saw my smile, he mimicked my shout: "Rescue!"

I realized I never asked his name. I pointed to myself and said, "Emily. Em-I-Lee."

He repeated it.

"Yes!" I pointed to each of us in turn. "Molly. Moll-Lee. Derek. Der-rick. And Viv."

He repeated each of their names, calling Viv "And Viv." I didn't correct him.

I pointed at him. "What…is…your…name?"

"Jacinto," he said.

"Jacinto." I wanted to hug him but not knowing his traditions, I refrained. Instead, I gave a slight bow and a big smile. "Nice…to…meet…you…Jacinto." Emotion needed no language; it was felt, and my smile was contagious.

Jacinto veered towards the jungle, and as he stepped into the overgrowth, we paused at the border. With no choice, we were once again swallowed inside the wall of green. Jacinto walked quickly and quietly, as if born to walk here. With him by my side, the jungle didn't feel ominous. Instead, it took on the aspect of welcome, a secret garden, even a luminous playground.

I tapped the man and mime-asked, "How…much…longer?" I used my two fingers to make a walking motion.

He spoke and I didn't understand a word. He pointed at the sun and then pointed a few degrees away from its location in the sky. He wasn't talking *distance*; he was talking time.

Molly asked, "What do you think, Emily?"

"I don't know. Maybe a few hours? The end of the day?"

Viv said, "I don't care. A day or two is fine. We're going home!" She suddenly cried. "I can't believe it. Home. It's real. It's really real."

Derek dragged behind, his hatchet at his side. He said to Viv, "What are you gonna miss most about this place?"

"Seriously? Not a damn thing."

Derek stopped. "What about the stars? Your star?"

Viv gave him a *oh, that's so cute* look and said, "They aren't going anywhere. Like you said, they're always there."

"But you'll never see 'em again. Not like this."

"Derek," she said. "Believe me, that's a good thing."

I turned to Molly, "What's the first thing you're going to do when you get back?"

"Sleep. I am going to sleep in my queen bed with a comforter and stuffed animals and just lie there forever and ever."

Viv said, "I am going to eat. Like, anything. Whatever it is. Chocolate cake, BBQ, ice cream, lobster bisque, the fattier, the better."

Viv was talking to me! She was talking normal!

"I'm going to take a long, hot shower," I said. "And stay there until my skin shrivels up."

"A shower! That's right," said Molly. "I'll do that first."

"Actually," Viv laughed, "I can't wait to use a proper toilet."

I thought of all the things I looked forward to: Chapstick, a cozy robe and slippers, Kleenex and nail clippers. Not the sexiest list, but definitely the most necessary.

I turned to Derek. "What about you, Derek? What's the first thing you're going to do?"

"What?"

"Home. What's the first thing you're gonna do when you get there?"

"I don't know." He seemed distracted.

"Derek? You all right?"

After a moment his eyes found me and he said, "Yes. I'm fine. Great, actually."

"Good."

With that, he got a bounce in his step, and I thought: there's the Derek I'd come to know. He radiated happiness, and now we could all share the good news as a group. He picked up speed as he passed us, walking quickly towards Jacinto.

Suddenly, Derek lifted the hatchet and with a wide baseball swing embedded it into Jacinto's neck. It took a moment for me to process what I was seeing. Red spurted from the man as he toppled to the ground with the wild boar. The hatchet raised again and again, the sick sounds of watermelon being sliced echoing around us. The man who was moving only seconds before now lay still, a splash of red against the wall of green. And through it all there was a bizarre smile on Derek's face; a happy grin that didn't belong.

It was only later I realized all of us were screaming.

CHAPTER TWENTY-SIX

I ran. My feet moved beneath my legs and I rushed through the green, tree branches flying past my face, my heart pounding in my ears, my breath frantic and shallow. I was so turned around, I didn't know where I was going, only away—faster, farther, gone.

Behind me, I heard the calls of a monster: "Emily! Emily!"

I was prey and though I darted every which way, I felt him gaining.

The image stuck in my mind: the hatchet slick with blood. The strain it took for Derek to wedge it out of the man's body before plunging it back. The piston-like repetition of the hatchet going up and down. A man's body that didn't look like a man anymore.

I wanted to stop and heave. I wanted to bawl my eyes out. I couldn't.

I had to go. Any direction, anywhere.

I ran and ran, panic infusing me. Panic confusing me.

I wasn't a person or name. I was movement.

Suddenly, I tripped. The world whirled past in a sickening blur and then it went black.

"Emily," a voice whispered to me. I opened my eyes. It was dark outside, and I couldn't see past a canopy of leaves. My vision blurred at the edges. Squatting next to me was Derek, his face calm and concerned. He rested his palm on my forehead. My head throbbed. I was lying down. Glancing at my sides, I was in a bamboo stretcher. Derek must've found me after I passed out. He must've carried me back here. Wherever here was.

I moved my hand to his and there on my forehead was a knot, thick and round. It hurt to touch.

"Gave yourself quite a lump. Looks like a small egg." He used a shredded red cloth to pat my head. "You're lucky I found you when I did. What if an animal found you first?"

Then I remembered. The cloth, I realized with horror, was from the man's Coca-Cola shirt.

"You killed him." My voice sounded disembodied.

I wanted him to say *what are you talking about? You must've dreamt that. He's right over there.* But all he said was, "It should heal in a few days."

I fell into a hole of sadness. For the native who died. For Derek who had clearly lost his mind. And for us, stuck in the jungle with him. "He was going to save us."

"I know."

"Why, Derek?"

"Why would I go back to the way it used to be, Em? Who would ever choose to go back to that life, if that's what you want to call it? I belong here. I fit. Do you know how that feels? To finally find a place where I can be myself?" Filth was trapped underneath his fingernails, and I wondered if the man's blood was mixed in with it.

"You belong back home."

"I killed a man. Back home, I'd go to jail, but here? It's survival of the fittest."

"No one would blame you. You're in shock. The crash, everything we've been through. You can still go home. It's not too late. I'll help you. I'll say whatever you want—"

"Emily." He gently shushed me. "I know exactly what I'm doing. I'm not crazy. In fact, this is—how do I say it?—the clearest I've felt in a long time." As if to illustrate his point, he took a long breath of air through his nose.

I shut my eyes, trying to shut him out.

"I know you don't understand, Em. I don't expect you to. But I want you to know something. Something I never told anyone. Remember the day after my prom videos went viral? All those porn pictures in my locker? I was going to kill myself that day. I'd had enough. I hated myself. I hated being Derek Wert. So I researched ways to...leave. I had the drugs. The plastic bag to put over my head. A motel room reserved. I had it all planned out. Even a note in my pocket. I went to school to say goodbye to my old life. But when you helped me, in the middle of all them laughing...it meant a lot. And then you went to prom with me. I couldn't believe it. I'm alive because of you."

"Then that man is dead because of me." Everything was tragic. So damned tragic. "Why didn't you just run off and let us go without you?"

"Because...." He paused for a few moments. "Whoever found you would never leave if they knew I was alive. My parents, they'd put out a reward. This place would be crawling with people, bounty hunters, fortune hunters. It'd never stop. But in a few days, the planes that are looking for us will stop. They'll call off the search." He looked up towards the sky. "Maybe they have already."

I couldn't cry. I was empty of everything except one thing, and it spread through my entire body, my entire being. "I hate you, Derek. You should've killed yourself. We would've all been better off."

He gave me a sad smile. "Then you wouldn't be alive today." He left some grubs and they wiggled on my chest. "Eat. They're good for you." He stood and walked away and I thought *this is what I get for being a good person.*

I stayed lying down, aware of my concussion, wondering where Viv was. Where was Molly? The jungle was loud and I couldn't hear conversation, and all around me was a kind of leaf-tent that Derek must've pieced together. There was movement everywhere—insects and dripping leaves and I felt as if I was swaying on a boat at sea. I yearned for stillness; I needed the world to stop so I could think. I wasn't hungry and let the grubs fall to the ground. I pushed myself up, feeling a vicious swell of nausea. It took a moment and the sensation passed. I stood on two feet and wobbled into the jungle.

It was dark, and I didn't like the dark. I saw the beds Derek had made, one for Viv and himself, the other for Molly. Molly saw me and got up. Derek watched lazily from his bamboo perch, totally unconcerned.

We moved to some bushes and I squatted. From a distance, it looked as if I was using the bathroom. I spoke to Molly in whispers. "What happened?"

"After you fell, he made a stretcher. And we dragged you here."

"What about the man?"

"Derek took his spear and his clothes and left his body. He said the animals would get him. There wouldn't be anything to find. Then he dug a hole, a deep one. And buried the clothes."

"And you guys? Has he…?" I didn't want to imagine what he could've done.

She shook her head. "That's the weirdest thing. He hasn't threatened us. He built the beds. Found us food. It's like nothing ever happened."

I looked past her at Viv, lying on the bamboo, her face turned away from us. "And Viv?"

"She hasn't said a word since."

I wanted to go over and comfort her, but I didn't know how Derek would react. Or Viv, for that matter.

I asked Molly, "Where are we?"

"I don't know…."

"I mean, how far are we from the road?"

Molly's face scrunched and she stopped herself from crying. "I don't know. I lost my sense of direction, everything's all messed up."

"Can you remember? Any guesses?"

Molly shook her head, and that's when the tears came.

"I'm sorry, Molly," and I hugged her.

"I didn't do anything. I was paralyzed. I couldn't move. I just sat there and watched as he…."

"There was nothing you could've done. Nothing."

She whispered even quieter, if such a thing was possible. "We're trapped here."

"We'll leave."

"We can't."

I understood with frightening clarity. We really were trapped. We needed Derek. We needed a murderer to survive. And he would never leave. We would never leave. I was going to be sick.

"We'll be okay," I lied.

"Will we?"

This would not be our destiny. We would not spend our lives here. I would make sure of that.

"I promise."

That night, back on my bamboo stretcher, I couldn't sleep. I plotted escape plans. There were always two things wrong: first, I didn't want to leave Viv behind. Or Molly for that matter. One person might be able to sneak off, but three? Second, the plans weren't really plans. They were the run-and-hope kind. Run and hope that I would find the road. Run and hope I would find the tribal village. Run and hope I wouldn't starve to death. Run and hope I wasn't going deeper and further into the jungle.

I didn't know what to do.

At least in camp, I had food. A semblance of shelter. I was safe. I was safer with Derek than I was without him.

Truthfully, I didn't want to go by myself. The more of us there were, the higher the chances somebody, somewhere might find us. Alone, I could wither and die and end up as lost as Nico, Ryan, and Jacinto.

I didn't want to die.

I didn't want to die alone.

Someone else, but not me.

In the morning, we woke and got up like normal, and I hated that it was becoming 'normal.' We emptied our bladders, put on mud masks, drank water, and ate grubs. Except this time Derek made sure to dismantle the beds, scattering their pieces randomly over the jungle floor, erasing any evidence that we'd been there. Then we were off, hiking. I didn't know where we were going, but Derek seemed to have a place in mind. I sensed wherever he was going was opposite the river, opposite the road, and opposite civilization. The noise amplified, the air seemed heavier, the topography denser.

We didn't speak.

When I tried to talk to Viv, she ignored me. Not out of fear, as I would've expected; she just *wasn't there*. Whatever used to be behind her eyes was gone.

"Viv," I said. "Say something."

She looked at me like a doll.

I shook her. "Say something."

Derek turned and said, "Something wrong, Em?"

Something wrong? I thought. Of course there's something wrong! Everything's wrong! But I held my tongue.

"No," I replied.

"Good. Then let's keep going. We've got a big day ahead of us."

Molly, Viv and I followed, saying nothing. Whatever hope we had felt the previous day was inverted, our bodies little husks, drained, brittle and dry, as if we could snap and crumble.

By the time night fell, we were deep under a canopy. There was no way to see the sky, nor for a plane to see us. Derek suddenly stopped.

"What do you think?"

No one replied.

"Seriously, what do you think?"

"Of what?" I said.

"Your new home."

"You mean the jungle?"

"No, I mean right here. We've been nomads since the crash. But this place is perfect. It's on high ground, so no floods. It's flat. We can clear out this area and I'll build a hut. Something sturdy. Picture it." He had the zeal of a prophet. "A roof over our heads. No more rain. No more wind. Hell, I'll even make an outhouse, so you guys'll have some privacy. There's plenty of bamboo, plenty of water vines. Now that I've got this," and he held the spear in his hands, "I can hunt. Even fish. What do you say?"

"That's nice, Derek." It was the first thing Viv had said all day.

"I'm glad you see the vision." He turned to me. "This is living off the land, off the grid, no pollution. Eating fresh, eating healthy." When I didn't comment, he added, "I know this has all been a shock, but we can make this work. I promise, on my honor to make it work. So, what do you say?"

I said, "On your honor as what?"

"A Boy Scout."

"Was murder part of the Boy Scout creed?"

Molly and Viv flinched. The air was heavy with silence.

"Emily, this is about freedom for all of us. But the past is something I won't tolerate."

I pressed him. "Won't tolerate *how?*"

Now it was Derek who tightened his hand around the spear. "Please don't make me do something I don't want to do."

I wondered exactly what that was.

"Emily." It was Viv. So she wasn't completely comatose. Almost imperceptibly, she shook her head. I got the message. I took comfort that Viv cared about me, if only a little.

Molly said, forcing cheer, "This place looks as good as any other."

"It's lovely," Viv said, and this seemed to get his attention.

"That's the spirit! So, who wants to help me build our home?"

Molly and Viv raised their hands.

We gathered bamboo, stalks and stalks of it. Making the home (I refused to call it 'our home') wouldn't happen overnight; it would take days. What else was there to do but help?

The more I watched the jungle floor transform into something approaching a structure, the more depressed I got. I should've been grateful to get out of the constant drizzle; to have a safe place from everything that was outside. Yet, every piece of bamboo we stitched together, every wall we created felt like one more brick on a prison of our making. This was our tombstone, our mausoleum.

I found myself wondering if Derek would devise a way to lock the door from the outside, trapping us when he went hunting. But he didn't need a lock to trap us; he did that by keeping his survival skills to himself. In the past, he'd been happy to point out which mushrooms were edible or not, or how to bend and use bamboo. He was a fountain of information, spouting trivia about biology and tips he'd learned while camping. Now when we asked about what kind of plants we could eat, he said, "Leave that to me." When we asked, "How far to the river?" He said, "Leave that to me." Our ignorance was our cage.

I said, "Let me help you get food so you don't have to do it all the time."

"I don't mind. It makes me feel more like a man."

"But I want to help."

"I appreciate it, Em, but I got it covered."

I battled the urge to sabotage the project. To slow us down. But the heat and humidity did that for us. Sabotage, I realized, would gain me nothing. If caught, it would only incense Derek.

So work we did.

And Derek rewarded us for it. Or punished us.

One night, after a day where I straggled behind, he only gave me half the food as everyone else: three mushrooms to Viv's six, (and because of her pregnancy, Molly's nine).

"Gotta earn your keep, Em."

The hours ran together because one was so much like the next. We didn't talk; we worked. The only sense of time passing was watching the progress of the hut. Oftentimes, I felt like I was living a nightmare rather than living. When Derek would go out searching for food, I found I was actually worried. He provided food, knowledge and life itself. What if he got sick? Hurt? Attacked by an animal? The worrying made me ill, not just the worry itself, but that fact that I was worried *about him*. I laughed. I was worrying about a murderer.

Another night passed, and Derek must've been satisfied with my work, for I earned a full meal. It was raw snake, stripped of its skin. It was chewy and rubbery and tasted like…amphibian? It was hard to tell, as I hated snakes—they were revolting creatures—and I swallowed the nubs of meat as fast as I could.

I asked him that night, with the roofless hut behind us, "Derek, I've been thinking. What if I left?"

"You mean here?"

"You could give me some mushrooms for the trip, and when I got rescued, I promise not to tell anyone about you. Or where you were. In fact, I'd go one better and tell them you were dead."

"Emily—"

"No one would ever know. Your parents. Your mother. I'd lie for you, Derek." Out of the corner of my eye, I saw Viv and Molly's face alight with something—hope? Or fear?

"I don't want to discuss this any more."

"I understand what you're doing. You can be happy here. You can trust me."

He slapped the ground and his eyes bored into mine. "I said I don't want to talk about this anymore! Do you understand?" He took a breath and calmed down. No one spoke. He tried to lighten the mood. "We should think of a name for our house. Casa something."

Casa hell, I thought.

"Emily, any ideas? You're the creative one."

"Casa Derek?"

He sighed. "It's for everyone. Not just me."

Molly said, "How 'bout Casa Selva? Don't quote me on it, but I think selva means jungle in Spanish."

"Not bad. But it's too obvious. We're already in the jungle. The hut is an escape—a home." We ate in silence a little longer and then he snapped his fingers. "I got it! What about Casa Shangri-La?"

Viv said, "I like the sound of that."

"Me, too," Derek replied. "Me, too."

That night, as I settled into bed next to Molly, I heard Viv in bed next to Derek. I didn't want to hear, but I couldn't help it. They'd grown closer over the last few days, not like any normal relationship, but more the way someone who adopts a stray animal. Viv gave affection for the simple fact that she got fed.

Viv whispered to him, "I think what you're doing is remarkable. If people could see you now, they'd know how special you are."

"You think so?"

"I know so."

I took a peek and saw Viv lightly rubbing her fingers over Derek's arm. Molly moved beside me and I could feel that she was watching, too.

"I'm sorry about what I said earlier. About my star and how it was a good thing I'd never see it. I love my star. I just knew I'd always have it, no matter where I was."

"It's okay," he said. "We're here now."

They were silent as Viv continued making patterns of her own design over his body.

"I always knew it was you, Derek. Watching me from outside."

"You did?" He suddenly turned shy. "You weren't mad?"

She paused. "It's nice to be wanted."

"I...don't know how that feels."

"What if I showed you?"

No, Viv. Don't do it.

"Showed me what?"

"What it feels like to be wanted." Her hand moved beneath his clothes, and his arms intertwined with hers.

"I've never...." he said.

"It's okay."

I shut my eyes.

I shut my eyes but could still hear.

I could still hear the rustling as their clothes came off. The sounds of hands on skin. Of breath and movement and the bamboo beneath them. Almost as quickly as it began, it ended with a short gasp.

CHAPTER TWENTY-SEVEN

There's something about signing your name on a document that you can't help but feel important. I'm legally a minor, so my mother signs, too. She told me earlier, "If this is a way to empower you, I'm all for it." She hands the document to Alan White.

I guess I'm officially making lemonade.

"Welcome to the family," Alan says and shakes my hand. "I'll get started right away fielding offers. How soon do you think you'll be ready to leave?"

My mother says, "The doctors say she's gonna be fine. The airline just wants to make sure she has the best care possible."

"The airline has an image to protect. So, maybe a couple days?"

"That seems awfully soon," I say. It's happening so fast. Promises of talk shows. Publishing houses. Hotel rooms and schedules, and of course, the promised money and opportunities down the line.

He shrugs sympathetically. "There's always another story around the corner. Gotta move while the iron is hot."

My mother looks at me. "Whatever you want, honey."

"I'd rather wait. Just a little. I'm not ready to travel."

My mom's hands go to her mouth. "Oh, Emily, I never thought of that. I'm sorry."

Alan quickly intercedes. "We'd hire a private bus to take her to New York, of course. Though getting on a plane would be a powerful symbol that you were moving on with your life."

Is that what I'm doing? Moving on with my life? "I am never getting on a plane again."

"I see." A slight frown appears on Alan's forehead. Then it's gone and his eyes sparkle. "What if we brought the interviews to you?" Off my quizzical expression, he says, "The shows can come here. Equipment, host and all. In fact...." He strolls around the room. "These are good optics. White background. Stark. Empty." He seems to be talking more to himself. "It creates this *yearning* for you to reach beyond it. People love a story. Something they can invest their hopes in. You're a mirror for them, don't you see? Hard-working girl tries to make good. Works at the local burger joint. Attends private school on scholarship. You're the American dream. And then it's tragically taken away. Yes, yes. This could work very well."

"But I don't...."

My mother gazes at me, and I hesitate to say it out loud, for it sounds too vain after all that's happened. "I don't look good. I still have scabs, and I'm too skinny."

"If you looked perfect, then people wouldn't care. You wouldn't connect. They want you to look like this. Then, when we do your book tour a year from now, people will see how far you've come. They'll feel like they're a part of the journey. Understand?"

"I guess so." But it all sounds so calculating.

"Good, good. This is going to be an exciting time. Your life's gonna change, Emily. It's gonna change in a big way. Just remember: you earned this. You deserve it."

I smile, trying to convince myself. I deserve something, all right, but I'm not sure this is it.

I had a fantasy that the gasp I heard from Viv and Derek's bed hadn't been the sigh of pleasure, but the sigh of Derek being stabbed to death by Viv. I opened my eyes and saw them together. There was no blood and no weapon.

It had been sex, not death. They rose from the bed, naked in the shafts of moonlight. Rather than being erotic, they were skeletal, like drugs addicts doing what needed to be done to score their next hit. They put their threadbare and filthy clothes back on. The bamboo creaked as they lay back down and Derek rolled over, his breath slowing and soon he was asleep.

I caught Viv's eyes. There had been a death, after all: a little bit of her soul.

In the morning, after Derek went off foraging, I pulled Viv aside. "Why'd you do that?"

"Do what?"

"You know what. You didn't need to, Viv."

She gazed at me with that blank look of hers. I hated seeing her so far away. Suddenly, my thought became action and I slapped her. I wasn't sorry. I needed Viv, not this other person who looked like her and simply took up space. Her cheeks blossomed red, and she suddenly appeared, that's the only way I can describe it. Her eyes flared and she rubbed her face.

"Don't ever hit me again, Em."

Anger was good. Anger was energy. I could harness that. "Why did you sleep with him?"

"Because you didn't."

"What's that supposed to mean?"

"Don't you get it? He'll listen to me. He'll get us out of here. I'll convince him. Because he will love me. He will do anything to make me happy. Maybe not right away, but soon. And when it's all over, when we're home, we can pretend this never happened." She sighed with disgust. "You ask me what I did? I *rescued us*."

I stood dumbfounded.

We were all heroes in our own way, heroes in the stories we told ourselves.

"I'm sorry, I had no idea."

Then she slapped me. "That's for Nico."

It stung. "I deserved that."

"That and more." The anger in her face subsided, and she began fading, the far-away person coming to the surface. I wondered which was real and which was the imposter.

I couldn't let her go. "Come back to me, Viv. You warned me not to make Derek mad. I know you still care. I'm sorry. I miss you. Come back to me."

Her eyes were dead. "Better get to work," she said. "Derek wanted this roof thatched before he got back." Viv turned from me and began the work of the day, days I'd stopped counting.

She was gone. She had been so close, but *chose* to drift. That was the most painful thing of all.

When Derek returned later that afternoon, we had finished the roof, and it was only a matter of putting it into place. The roof was large, like a big, woven quilt of green and awkward to move. The four of us were able to rest it on the supporting walls and then push it on top and flush with the sides. I thought of the Amish raising a barn, and the pride they probably felt. I felt no such pride. I would've set fire to the hut if I could.

We picked up our beds and moved them inside. It was dark and dank, except where spots of sunlight poked through from tiny holes, akin to fake stars affixed to a ceiling. The hut looked like an abandoned cabin you might find in the outback, rickety and empty, but for us, it was shelter. Viv started tearing up, and I wasn't certain if it was because it was shelter, or the fact that it was so sub-par to any definition of normal living. There was something worse about it being like a home, because no matter how we might improve on it, it would never be one.

"I can't believe it. It's like…." Derek looked out the front door. "It's like we're settlers in the Wild West. Homesteaders." He ran his hands over the bamboo poles, feeling their stability, seeing how they held against his weight. To his credit, they did. The structure was solid. The floor, too, was stamped dirt and in time would dry.

"This is only the beginning, you know?" He circled the hut testing each wall. "Course, after the first big rain, it'll probably leak. But we'll patch it up and soon enough it'll be fairly water-tight."

"In the coming days, I'll build the outhouse over there." He pointed a few yards away. "You won't have to walk far. Then I'll build a fish station over there so we don't attract any critters. I know it's not much, but in time…. Maybe we can whittle down some wood and make plates. Even forks and spoons. Hell, we can put a table right here. We can have dinner. Lots to do. Lots to do."

He looked at Molly. "I nearly forgot! You can give birth here! We'll have an all-natural birth. How beautiful will that be? It'll be a child of the world. No citizenship. Just ours."

Molly seemed horrified by the idea.

He motioned for us. "Gather 'round."

We did as he asked and faced each other in a circle in the center of the room. Viv avoided my eyes.

Derek said, "It's like we're a family." He patted Molly's belly. "A growing family." He looked at us each in turn. There were tears in his eyes. "It's my great pleasure to welcome you to Casa Shangri-La."

CHAPTER TWENTY-EIGHT

That night, we slept for the first time "indoors." The walls helped me feel more secure, though they did nothing to diminish the noise from outside. Screeches and the drone of insects drifted through the doorway, seemingly echoing in the closed-off space. Across from me were noises of a different sort. Now that Derek had a taste of carnal knowledge, he was eager to learn more. If Viv wasn't careful, Molly wouldn't be the only one pregnant around here.

This was insanity. Derek, with his utopian fantasy, and Viv, I didn't know what to think. We would eventually leave and when she got back home there'd be no way to "forget anything had happened." Something *had* happened; something she never would've done under any other circumstance. Was that courage or victimization? Derek might fall in love with her, but he would never go back to society. Why would he? Everything he wanted was here. A girlfriend he could control; a girlfriend who would never leave. He was king, Viv his queen, and we were his subjects. No one gives up position and power. Not without a fight.

Unless Viv needed comforting herself. People in pain sought release. Maybe Derek was her answer, and if so, who was I to judge? If I was honest with myself, I needed comforting, too.

As much as I held out hope, I was beginning to doubt if we'd ever be rescued. Derek was probably right. Someone somewhere had called off the search. All evidence pointed to total disaster: no survivors. The mission would turn from rescue to recovery, and after that, nothing. No one searches for ghosts.

Viv and Derek were very much alive, though. Molly and I could've slept outside to avoid being so close to them, but Derek didn't last long and soon he was asleep. I wanted to reach out and whisper to Viv. To tell her again she was my best friend, how I didn't want to lose her, and I missed her dearly. She wasn't alone in her pain.

I never did, and I regret it every day.

Sometime in the night, I rolled over, surprised to find more room on the bed. Molly was gone, the bamboo cool to the touch. She wasn't inside the hut. Across from me, Viv and Derek slept, hatchet and spear by his side. I stepped off the bed and onto the dirt floor. Nico had run off like this, and he'd taken food. But there was nothing to steal, as Derek foraged for fresh food every morning.

Molly didn't seem like the type to run away and definitely not at night. The jungle was difficult enough to navigate during the day, but when dark descended, it was a whole other world. I stood near the doorway and heard the sounds of crying.

It had to be Molly. I knew exactly how she felt. I thought of going outside to comfort her, but she'd left to get some privacy. I wanted to respect that.

I don't know what kept me from going back to bed, other than I was already up. Molly's cries continued to float in the air, blending with the jungle's cacophony. I waited a few minutes until I could listen no more. Like sonic breadcrumbs, I followed the sound of her tears, growing closer and closer until I saw her near a tree. When she saw me, her eyes were frantic, her face wet with tears, and she quickly turned away as if I'd caught her doing something wrong.

"Molly?"

She hid behind a tree. "I'm fine, Emily. Just stay there."

"What's wrong?"

"Nothing."

Going to the bathroom in the jungle hadn't been an issue; any vanity we had disappeared as soon as we entered the wall of green. I'd seen every bodily function and nothing could surprise me. So why was Molly acting so strange?

"Are you hurt?"

"Please, Emily, leave me alone."

I stood only a few feet away and waited for a sign. I thought if Molly wanted to be alone, let her. But the tremor in her voice made me think otherwise.

I peered around the tree and Molly shrunk from me. Her pants were down, but she wasn't using the bathroom. There was something on her thighs. I thought she must've had diarrhea in the night and rushed outside and was now embarrassed. Molly reached out as if to keep me away and I saw the same dark substance on her hand.

"Molly, what happened?"

"Go away!"

I realized the substance wasn't what I thought. She was bleeding. The dark substance was blood. I couldn't imagine suffering a miscarriage alone, away from home, away from support. "Molly, are you okay?" I tried to comfort her, and she shied away from me even more.

"Don't. Just don't." She couldn't meet my eyes.

"You're hemorrhaging. We've gotta get you help!"

I turned to wake the others. If we didn't stop the bleeding, Molly might die. I wouldn't let that happen.

"Emily, wait!"

"You need help. I promise, we'll do what we can—"

"It's not a miscarriage."

I stood, stupid, processing what she'd said.

I'd been played for a fool. She'd never been pregnant. This was her *period*. "Were you ever?"

She didn't answer which was answer enough. She asked, "Do you have anything?"

I shook my head.

Molly said, "Will you tell the others?"

"No. But they'll find out eventually."

I didn't need to ask why she'd made it up. She wanted preferential treatment: more food, less work, understanding when she lagged behind; compassion. Hell, I wanted compassion, too. I wasn't mad. I understood the things people did to survive.

But if she'd lied about this, she may have lied about something else.

I asked, "Were you ever with him?"

She shook her head. "I was tired. I didn't want to walk anymore. It just popped in my head. And then you all started asking questions. It was easier to say it was someone on the plane."

So her relationship with Johannes had always been a lie. Rather than get angry, I was flooded with relief. He loved me, I thought. He really loved only me.

I'm sorry, Johannes. I'm sorry I doubted you.

I wanted to cry.

I'd been loved, truly and totally. I should've trusted him.

My body trembled and I had to stop from bawling. Being angry was easier than mourning. Being dead inside was easier than confronting death. Sadness fell against me. I caught my breath, trying to maintain my composure.

Molly began wiping herself with leaves, trying to clean what she could.

"Why him?" I asked. "You could've picked anybody."

"Because I had a crush on him. He was the only guy who was kind. Who encouraged me. Who *saw* me." She crumpled up the leaves and tossed them into the green. "It's silly…but I loved him."

"I understand more than you know."

"I know," she said. "I saw the way you two were with each other."

"What do you mean?"

"The day in his office after you left. Remember?"

"But nothing happened."

"Nothing needed to. I just *knew*." I was about to speak, and she interrupted. "Don't deny it, Emily. My fantasy was crushed. I felt so stupid. I was this close to picking up the phone and telling everybody about you and him. About everything."

"Why didn't you?"

"Because after I thought about it…he was my *teacher*. And you were with him. I felt bad for you."

"Felt bad for me?"

Molly nodded and pulled up her pants.

"What are you talking about?" I said. "You're the one who lied to get sympathy you didn't deserve."

"You don't get it. I may be fat, but I know I'm fat. I know how people look at me. But you? You make me realize how lucky I am."

I didn't understand.

"You want me spell it out for you?"

I was stunned and my silence only emboldened her.

"You grew up with a single mom never knowing who your father was. It's psychology 101. Guys in school like you, but either you don't notice, don't care or don't want them. Maybe it's all three. The *one* guy who catches your eye is a teacher. You're just a cliché."

"He's not my father's age."

"Doesn't matter. He's not *your* age." She wiped her hands on the ground. "He's probably everything you wish your father was. Instead of who your father probably is."

I wanted to hit her. I wanted to hit her so bad.

I didn't believe a word of it. Love was love, no matter the age. Molly was just jealous, lashing out. I didn't know much about her family other than her father worked all the time and was never home. She was probably the one with daddy issues.

I pointed at the hut. "I could just tell them the truth."

Molly said, "On second thought, maybe I did have a miscarriage." She smiled. "Thanks for coming out in my time of need." Then she walked back to the hut and I was alone.

In Johannes' crushing absence, soon it was me crying outside in the dark.

CHAPTER TWENTY-NINE

I was alone. Viv, Molly and Derek were gone, lost to the jungle, lost forever.

I walked. I had walked for so long. I had a vague sense of direction. The sun rose in the east and set in the west. I tried heading south, but god only knew what direction I really went. The jungle looked the same no matter how far I traveled, and I feared I was going in circles, always coming back to the same spot. I'd run and hoped, walked and hoped, staggered and hoped, and my hope was dying.

I hadn't eaten in days. Hadn't had water save a few drops I licked from leaves. I was becoming part of the jungle.

Every step I took was effort. Lift, step, move and repeat. I was reduced to my essence. I'd been boiled for so long, there was only the tiniest shred of life left.

I wanted to stop.

I wanted to lay under a tree and sleep.

It all seemed so futile.

But I would not die here. I would not die in this place. I would not allow everything that had happened to be lost to history, lost to the soil.

Time was meaningless. The sun rose, the sun set; there was day and there was night, but the measurements between were nothing.

At some point, I didn't daydream; I didn't think. I was aware of a strange sensation: I moved, proven by the distance I covered, but I did so without conscious effort. Rather than feel alarmed, I liked not having to be present, not having to feel every strain. I was calm, the waves of my mind placid. I moved pleasantly by some other source, floating like a bird over the undergrowth. The jungle was circus-like, a kaleidoscope of bursting color, and for all I knew I was crossing into another plane of existence.

There was brightness ahead, light streaming from beyond the trees. It shone on me, and I thought of all the stories about near-death experiences and how they must be true. Death was coming. My life was drawing to a close. I wasn't afraid. The light drew closer and encompassed me, growing brighter and more intense. I couldn't see anything beyond the light and noise; it obliterated everything, making the leaves sway. Even the wet mud rippled beneath my feet.

The light shifted from my eyes and there in the sky was a helicopter, a man rappelling down with a kind of stretcher attached. I thought I was dreaming. The man landed on the ground and approached. I embraced him and never wanted to let go. As he bundled me into the stretcher, he asked in broken English, "Is there anyone else with you?"

I reached out into the depths of the jungle and I couldn't feel Viv's spirit. We'd been so close, but I knew in my heart she was dead. It was impossible to think of life without her in it.

I shook my head. "I'm the only survivor."

Then he gave a signal and the stretcher was hoisted up and I rose in the air, watching as the jungle receded below me. I rose parallel to the tall trees and finally above their canopy, seeing the beauty of their flat tops stretching into darkness, this lawn of green. Like a tendril of smoke, I left the soiled world behind and drifted into the sky.

CHAPTER THIRTY

My story is over. My journal is complete. There is nothing else to write. The journal entries I've written are what the world will read. I've never written anything as long, or as emotionally draining, and yet, now that it's over, rather than feel relief, I feel hollow. There is nothing to celebrate. I've tried my best to capture the misery we experienced, but in the end they're only words. They can convey only so much and not enough.

In the hospital, the camera crews left, the lights packed up, the electrical cords running like snakes on the floor rolled up and put away. Not more than an hour ago, there was a talk show host in this very room, a woman I had seen tons of times when flipping through channels. I know people on TV exist in real life, but to have them sit across from you, focused 100% on you is…surreal. She's talked to movie stars and presidential candidates and she was talking to *me*. I even had a hair and makeup person, though Alan made sure they didn't "pretty me up" too much. He wanted, as he called it, "the truth to shine through." Being on camera, I became self-conscious about how I spoke, the way my face looked, whether I blinked too little or too much. I didn't even remember my answers, though Alan and my mother told me afterward I'd done great.

"You were the perfect blend of humble and strong," he said. "Keep it up!" I didn't know how to take his praise: I wasn't an athlete. I was a survivor from a plane crash. The next few days would bring interview after interview, one a day, sometimes two. That is the schedule. I worried I would say the same things so much I'd start to sound rehearsed. He told me not to worry.

My mother tells me there's talk of scholarships in the names of the deceased at Riverdale Academy. The school promises to increase the number of underserved students. "At least," she says, "something good came from it." She's been doing that recently; reminding me of all the good things that have happened in the wake of the crash. The outpouring of concern, new airline safety initiatives, a reminder to live life instead of walking through it. As if all those things balance out tragedy. I'd rather nothing good happened if I could erase my memories. My mom says, "Once the interviews air, more people will want to help. It may mean a college scholarship. Offers for internships or jobs. Choices, honey. Choices you never had." Just as Alan had predicted.

I don't care about any of it. I don't care at all. All my life I wanted to be special. Here it is, offered on a silver platter—The Girl Who Survived—and it makes me sick.

At night when I see my mother sleeping on the chair across from me, I can tell she's changed. There isn't the scent of cigarettes wafting from her hair. She's not taking Ativan anymore. Either that, or she's taking much less, tapering her doses. She doesn't have a glazed donut look in her eyes. And yes, she and I are talking more. But overall, she's been the one most affected by the crash: she's been the one to change for the better. In her life, the crash is her Before and After moment, the piece of the puzzle that will motivate her to *carpe diem* her lemons into lemonade.

Since the crash, I think I've gotten worse. Or maybe the crash revealed who I really am.

After my time in the jungle, I finally understand my mother. I understand why she kept reaching for a pill to make life better: because life is too much to bear. The lies and selfishness, disappointment and loneliness, they're too hard to deal with on your own. It's too bad, 'cause now that I finally understand her, she's changing.

It kills me to see her off Ativan, because it only proves how awful I really am. She is facing life as it is while I hide. I hide behind lies; I hide behind feelings people place on me, like sympathy or courage, blessed or special.

I am none of those things.

My counselor wanted me to write things down so that I could make sense of what happened. I took her advice and tried to make sense of things—not of what happened, but of what I did.

The Emily Duran who emerged from the jungle was broken. I remade her, stitching her back together piece by piece.

I rewrote my life.

I wrote a story about a character named Emily Duran who looked and talked like me, but was so much better. The story was the version of myself I *wanted* to be. The version I so wished I was.

But I'm not.

I thought writing my story—and that's what it was—a story, not a history, would make things better. By writing, I could erase the past and create a new one. But in lying, line after line, page after page, it made me feel worse. I kept writing thinking *Finish it. Finish and everything will fall into place.*

It hasn't.

I finished the story, but it seems the story isn't finished with me.

I cannot escape the truth.

I cannot escape my guilt.

I cannot escape *myself* no matter how hard I try.

"I'm sorry, Mom." She sleeps, probably not hearing, but I continue anyway. Someone needs to know the truth. I need to unburden myself before I sink into a hole and never return. "I'm a liar and a fraud, and I'll tell you what really happened."

After crying myself empty in the dark, I walked back to the hut. Molly was asleep on the cot. I was disgusted by her lie and disgusted at myself. Disgusted by everyone, at how we devolved. We weren't starting over; we were stepping backwards.

I crept up to Derek's cot. He and Viv slept, releasing small snores. On the floor rested the spear. I reached down and picked it up, feeling its weight and pointed the sharp end towards Derek's body. I mentally played out the movements it would take to kill him; pulling my arm back like cocking a trigger and thrusting it into his kidneys, feeling the resistance of his body, pull out and repeat. There would be blood. There would be screaming. But the nightmare would be over.

Or would it?

I heard Molly stirring. I looked over, waiting to see her eyes on me, waiting to hear her gasp, setting off a chain reaction that would wake everyone up. But her eyes stayed closed. Then Derek stirred and changed his body position. I watched as he moved on the bed, eyes shut, getting comfortable, reminiscent of a baby in a crib, turning from his side to face-side up. Was it a sign? I could easily pierce his heart.

Is this how Derek felt on the night he stood over Nico? The jungle brought out something, almost daring us to give in to our darkest desires.

I held the spear. It would be so easy.

Too easy.

A voice in my head asked me: *Who's fault is it that you're still here?*

Yours.

You can leave at any time.

Who is there to stop you?

I placed the spear back on the floor. I was a coward, but I was no murderer.

In the morning, as we all got up, I didn't say anything about Molly's condition. It wasn't my problem anymore. In fact, my problems were less and less about other people, and more about me. I needed to get out of here. I kept waiting for something to happen, for someone to rescue us, for a spaceship to land and teleport me out of here. It wasn't happening; it would never happen. The more I waited, the more I feared I would become paralyzed and dependent on Derek, worried about him to the point where I would start protecting him, equating our survival with his.

I would leave. But not without Viv, no matter how she felt about me now. I would prove my loyalty and we would be friends again. I would make sure of it.

Derek said, "So, how'd everybody sleep?"

Viv said, "Good."

Derek teased, "Only good? Or great?"

Viv smiled; I cringed.

Derek began his morning ritual: using the bathroom, rinsing his face and drinking from a water vine. He'd found safe plants to rub on his teeth in place of toothpaste. He was becoming a regular Medicine Man. After he was done, he picked up the makeshift hatchet and spear and said, "I'm heading out." That's when I caught up to him.

"I'm coming with."

He stopped and looked at me quizzically. "Why?"

"I need mushrooms."

"I'm getting mushrooms."

"I'm getting mushrooms for myself, Derek." I could've chosen not to say anything, but I feared if I didn't say it out loud I wouldn't follow through. My own fear and dependence would hold me back. I needed to make my leaving real. And maybe in some weird way, I thought he'd be like the Derek I knew from Burger King, the Derek who would talk to me. The Derek who might actually come back with me. "I'm getting them and then I'm leaving."

I expected an outburst.

He was quiet for a moment, and then a smile crossed his lips. "Always keeping me on my toes, aren't you? Seriously, I'll be back with plenty."

I grabbed him. "I'm not kidding."

He could sense my seriousness and he grew serious, too. "You're not coming with me."

"I won't be here when you get back."

He scanned the area, making sure we were alone. "You're taking off with no food. No way of getting food. You realize that's suicide, right?"

"It's called escape."

By now, we'd caught the attention of Viv and Molly. They watched from the hut, pretending not to.

"From what?"

I was stunned. "What do you think? This. You. All of it."

He seemed genuinely shocked. "I never stopped you."

"'Don't make me do something I don't want to do.' You said that. You said that while holding a spear."

"I meant don't make me lose you as a friend. You took that as a threat?"

I couldn't believe his rationale. "You withheld food from me!"

"Because you weren't doing your fair share! What kind of message does that send to everyone if you slack off?" He calmed down. "This is your home. *Our* home. I just thought if I wasn't going back, there was no point in talking about how things used to be." He gazed off into the jungle. "I wanted us to be happy here. No pressure to achieve. No worries about making it into college. Leaving the whole two-kids-and-a-mortgage behind. Just us. Our own tribe."

He saw I wasn't convinced. He motioned towards Viv and Molly. "What about them?"

"I haven't told them anything." The truth was as soon as he gave me food and left, I was taking Viv with me, whether she wanted to or not. I would knock her unconscious and drag her if I had to.

"You can do what you want, Emily. There's no shackles on your feet."

Was I always free to go? Or was he playing mind games? "I need your help. I need food."

He took his time, glancing between me and them. "You can go." He added, "If you're really not here when I get back, I'll miss you. Good luck." He hugged me so tight I could smell the sweat and grime on his skin. For a split second, I thought he might stab me.

But he didn't.

In my ear, he said, "If you're rescued, tell them. Tell 'em I'm gone." Then he kissed me on the cheek and said cryptically, "I know what I've done. Do what you have to."

He didn't try to stop me. Not by force. But by withholding help. Out here it was the same thing.

He turned and something snapped in me. I would not be abandoned. I would not be trapped. I was so tired of this place. I'd seen too much death, too much mindless death. One more wouldn't make a difference. I reached down and picked up the first thing I saw—a rock. I brought it up and bashed it with all my strength down onto his head. I heard a sickening thud and he fell to the ground. I didn't look at his face, I simply repeated the motion and brought the rock down against his temple, and the softness of his skull gave way.

I was right.

There was blood. There was screaming. But I was wrong about one thing: the nightmare had only just begun.

CHAPTER THIRTY-ONE

"What have you done? What have you done?!" Viv was a wildcat, tearing towards me. She fell towards Derek and cradled his head in her lap. My body shivered, a strange energy infusing it. I couldn't tell if it was fear or exhilaration. I didn't know what I felt—regret, remorse, revenge? Maybe all three. Maybe none. I killed a man. I killed my friend. The man I knew from prom lay in the dirt, his eyes open to the sky. See what you've done, I wanted to shout. See what you made me do? Is this how you wanted to die?

This isn't who I was supposed to be!

I thought of his last words: *I know what I've done. Do what you need to.*

He wanted me to kill him. He wanted me to put him out of his misery. That's what I chose to believe. He never would've gone back to society and he knew it. This made him legend; this made him myth.

He made me his assassin. His murderer.

I felt crazy. Insane. My vision pulsed, and I realized it was my heartbeat in my eyes.

Maybe I knew all along this is what had to happen to get Viv to leave. She never would've left with me, not without a reason. Now I'd given her one. We were free. I had rescued her.

Viv gently moved a strand of hair out of his face. Maybe in the process of sleeping with him she'd grown to care for him. Her jeans were wet with his blood, and she sat, unmoving.

At least he seemed at peace.

Molly slowly stepped behind me. I couldn't decipher the look on her face. Fear? Shock? Or gratitude that I had done the hard thing when no one else could? She asked no questions, and I took her silence as tacit agreement.

Viv said quietly, her voice quivering, "He was falling in love with me."

I think in her grief it was the other way around.

"Viv," I said. "He was never going to leave."

"He was…."

"He was never going to leave—"

"I would've made him. I would've convinced him."

"He was going to die here. No matter what you did. No matter how many times you slept with him."

"You didn't give me a chance."

Viv didn't cry; she held him, rocking him in her lap. Moments passed and I kept irrationally thinking the police would come. Sirens would sound in the distance. Someone would help us. Someone had to help us before we disintegrated.

Viv said, "I didn't want it to be like this. It didn't need to be." She softly moved Derek's head from off her lap. "You killed him."

"Don't you see? We're free. I saved us, Viv. I saved you."

Her energy shifted from mourning to anger. "Don't bring me into this. He wasn't stopping you."

"He stopped us as soon as he killed that man."

"And killing Derek makes a difference?"

"He was a murderer."

Viv's eyes were cold. "So are you." There was a hardening between us, a wall of cement growing firmer with each passing second. "And now you've sentenced us to starve."

I couldn't believe she didn't see the truth. "Viv, we're going to leave. We're going to choose a point in the distance and keep walking towards it until we get out of here. We're going home now. Don't you see that?"

"You murdered him, Emily." Viv reached out and picked up the hatchet. Her whole body shook.

"What are you doing?"

She stood and faced me, and I was scared. She hadn't been acting herself. She was capable of anything.

"I slept with him, Emily. I let him inside of me. Do you think I *wanted* to do that?"

"No one asked you to!"

"Because I didn't want to kill him! And now it's all for nothing!" She waved the hatchet in front of her. "You didn't need to do it! He didn't have a weapon! He wasn't threatening you! He had his back turned! You could have run off!" She was hysterical now. Whatever dam of stress she'd been keeping bottled up, broke. "You're a coward! A coward and a killer!"

I had to keep this contained. I had to control the situation. "Viv, you're not thinking right."

"*I'm* not thinking right?"

"Please, just put it down."

"He was your *friend*."

"Viv, you're my friend. My best friend. Please." I approached her and she slashed the hatchet at me.

"Stay away from me!"

"Viv, listen to me! Listen to me!"

I stepped towards her and that's when she cut me. The hatchet sliced my arm, not deeply, but enough to bleed. In that moment of shock, there was an absence of sound, beyond silence, and there might've been space to make things right, to calm the waters, but the moment ended too quickly. The blood seemed to scare her. She looked at the hatchet, this weapon in her hand and dropped it like a burning object. She found me—a stranger to her—and then turned and ran.

"Viv, stop! Stop!"

I chased after her, but that only fueled her paranoia.

"Viv! Please! Come back! Come back!"

Viv scurried like prey and driven by adrenaline and fear, she was soon out of sight. She was all I had left. I stood in the middle of wherever the hell I was, watching the leaves she'd run through fall back to stillness, and it was the last time I would ever see her.

I waited in the jungle. If there were footsteps, they were buried under an avalanche of sound. If there were tears, they were lost in the drizzle of rain. I thought I could track her by following her footprints in the mud, but if I went too far from where I came I would get lost. I shouted her name over and over and got no response. Above me, trees swayed, their branches and leaves like a wicked creature, mocking my efforts. One moment Viv was in my world, my best friend, my confidant, and the next she was gone. Disappeared. I could not lose her. She was an appendage, part of my identity as much as my fingers and toes. Without her, I was nothing.

I shouted until I was hoarse. "Viv! Come back!"

I staggered back to the hut, hoping Viv had returned by a circuitous route, hoping she would understand. I imagined us hugging. She would cry and we would be sisters bound by blood. Our lives would stretch toward weddings and maids of honor, closer to each other than any husband.

But when I arrived, there was only emptiness.

She wasn't there.

She hadn't come back.

Viv was a city girl through-and-through. There would be no way she could survive. Watching her run off was as good as a death sentence. She'd left me. She'd left me to die by herself.

My own best friend didn't trust me. The last thing on her face had been horror. She'd been terrified. If I had passed a puddle of water, I would've looked at myself to see if I had changed. I felt the contours of my face, and they were the same. Whatever scared Viv was not how I looked, but what I did.

I killed Derek. I took a life. His life.

Was Viv right? Was I a murderer?

I didn't know anymore. I shut my eyes, losing myself in darkness.

I was too tired to stay awake, too distraught to sleep; I existed between extremes: freedom and captivity, the present and the past.

Molly stood near the doorway to the hut. She said, "I didn't know if you'd come back." It was she who rushed and hugged me. "I'm sorry, Emily. I never meant any of the things I said. Don't leave me. I can't make it on my own. Please, don't leave."

I never liked Molly and still didn't. She offered nothing in the way of skills or survival, but I would not be so callous to toss her aside. Instead, I would become her savior. I looked at her red, tear-streaked face and said, "I won't."

"What about Derek?" Off my confused look, Molly explained. "His body."

I didn't give it a second thought. "Leave it."

Molly nodded. Whatever I told her, I was certain she would do. I could play a game of Simon Says and she would do everything.

"We're leaving now."

She didn't nod. She just followed, a puppy behind her master.

Molly and I walked and walked. She never complained. She didn't even ask what had happened to Viv. For all Molly knew, I had killed her. I could sense Molly's fear. Not just of the jungle, but of me. I told her: we won't stop; we won't sleep; we will move until we find help or until we can't move anymore. We didn't waste energy with conversation. Every ounce of life was spent in motion.

I never did see the road again. I must've gone in the wrong direction. But it was too late to backtrack. By the time it was getting dark, we spotted a river. Whether it was the same from days ago, I didn't know. At least it was a landmark.

I pointed across the river and said to Molly, "There. Do you see them?"

She squinted. "The mushrooms?"

It was too far to see if they were the edible or poisonous kind, but they were sprinkled across the shore like a field of creamy flowers. To me they looked just as beautiful. "I say we cross and eat, then take as many as we can. What do you think?"

"If you think we can."

"We're gonna need to eat. Can't be too deep, right?"

"No," Molly said. But I saw the hesitancy on her face.

I tightened my shoelaces and then rolled my jeans into the sides of my shoes. Hopefully, it would act as a barrier against leeches. I stepped into the river and the water was cold. I tiptoed further. The water went up to my ankle, then my calves, knees and finally up to my waist. It was brownish and smelled like salt. Rather than feel cleansed, the water only made me feel dirtier. Molly was right behind me. The cold intensified as we waded towards the center and we shivered, two human bobbers floating on muck.

My feet bounced on the mud below, and the closer I got to the mushrooms, the hungrier I became. I could taste their earthy goodness, my stomach waiting for sustenance.

The river's current pushed us and we trudged against it. Step by step I walked, and suddenly, the bottom dropped out. The river became very deep. Fear took over as I tried to step back to gain purchase, but the current dragged me. I treaded water and shouted to Molly to be careful, but it was too late.

She stepped into the deep, and the current took her, too.

I kept my gaze on the shore and swam towards it. No matter how much the current wanted to pull me away, I was like a plane in turbulence, only focused on my destination.

Behind me, Molly screamed my name.

We were so weak. Every stroke took effort, and energy leaked from my body. I fought the urge to give up, to let go. The water enticed me, a giant womb, as if whispering *come to me, come back home. You belong here.* Water splashed in my face, blurring my vision. The shore was only yards away. The current was stronger now, very strong, and I couldn't move. My feet were stuck. I wasn't moving at all.

That's when I knew: this was no current.

It was Molly; she had grabbed my foot.

She was behind me, flailing, her face no longer human, but a creature screaming, filled with panic, her mouth open, trying to breathe, but the more she tried, the more water she inhaled. It was a vicious cycle, and her fingers were like a vice on my shoe.

I was so weak.

"Molly, let go! You're gonna drown us! Let go!"

She was too scared; that's all she was now: pure panic. I couldn't make out the sentences she said, only fragments.

I couldn't save her unless I saved myself. I kicked against her, trying to break free. I inhaled a mouthful of water and coughed. Molly was taking me down with her. I went under, water filling my ears, all sound going mute, air bubbles releasing to the surface, and came back up. I fought against her, and the more I fought, the tighter she held on.

I thrashed and we were two whirlpools.

The sounds she made were all garbled.

She was no longer Molly; she was a monster.

I had no choice.

I would survive.

I kicked at her, hitting her in the face with my free foot. Once, twice, until I heard the snap of her nose and I was free. I didn't look back. I took off for shore.

Almost there.

I spit out water from my mouth.

Another stroke.

I found traction on the river floor and four-legged myself onto land. I was soaked, out of breath and fiercely tired. The edges of my vision blurred and finally came into focus. I gasped for air, spending moments coming to a normal rhythm.

I heard no human sounds.

I moved my head. Molly lay face down, floating on the water's surface, easing down the river with a bizarre tranquility, as if a small blanket had been thrown overboard, and it drifted, rippling on the current, further and further away.

CHAPTER THIRTY-TWO

There were mushrooms on shore. Loads and loads of them, edible and safe, and I gorged myself. They were at the base of trees, spread out, a treasure trove of food, gold at the end of a rainbow. I never won anything, no awards, no lottery, nothing, but I won food, and it felt wonderful. A vicious thought intruded: you could've saved her. You could've saved Molly.

No, I argued with myself, she would've killed me. She would've drowned us both.

Did you really need the mushrooms?

Yes, I thought, and chewed.

How can you just sit there and eat?

"What do you want me to do?" I asked to no one. "I can't do anything." Not anymore.

You killed them both.

I yelled into the sky. "I killed them so that I could live! Is that so wrong? What else was I supposed to do? It's not my fault. It's not my fault!"

I thought: I have survived childhood; I will survive here. No one will drown me. Not my mother. Not Molly. No one will ever drown me. No one will ever take me down with them.

I ate until I could eat no more.

I rose from the ground, sopping wet and hewed close to the river.

I kept repeating to myself: the river leads to the ocean. The river leads to the ocean.

I drifted like a sleepwalker, walking for who knows how long. Days came and went. At some point, I had to veer from the river, as it became impossible to walk near it. Rocks and sudden drops became too hard to cross. I was back in the jungle, my old friend and nemesis, and it seemed to whisper *you will never leave*. Snakes and spiders kept their distance. I was one of them, a creature of this place.

I walked through daylight; I walked through nighttime. I stopped for nothing. Not food or drink. Not to use the bathroom. I was no longer scared of the dark. I was the unknown in this place. I was capable of anything. My sense of self fell away. I didn't know who I was. I fought to remember my name.

I am Emily Duran. I am Emily Duran.

I said those words over and over until they became meaningless, just sounds in my head. I said them to the point of ridiculousness, to where forming the words on my mouth felt odd, until language itself felt foreign. Alien. Like me.

I simply *was*. I existed. Sounds fell away, and I walked and walked.

I became a ghost haunting these woods. I had no substance; no hunger, no thirst, no desire.

I stopped feeling anything at all.

I thought I was dying.

That's when I saw the light. The bright light. It was Death, come to claim me.

When the helicopter medic asked me if there was anyone else with me, I hesitated.

Was this real or was I creating a conversation in my head? It took me a moment to process there was someone standing in front of me, an actual physical presence and not a hallucination. Nico, Ryan, Molly and Derek were gone.

What about Viv, I thought to myself. She could still be alive.

This wasn't who I was supposed to be.

I wanted a clean slate.

I'm no murderer.

I wanted to put this all behind me. Bury it in a big hole and never look back.

I would live and tell the story of who I was <u>meant</u> to be.

In that moment, less than seconds, I crystalized who I was: I chose between the past and the future, between who I was and who I would be.

I shook my head. "I'm the only survivor."

If my mother is awake and listening, she shows no sign of it. Her breathing is calm, rhythmic and deep. I whisper, "I was so angry at you for never being around, for being weak, but I'm so much worse. I'm a murderer. I'm a murderer and I'm being hailed as a hero. What do you think of that?"

She doesn't respond.

The guilt has been eating away at me, a disease with no cure but the truth.

"I wrote the story of what happened to me. The story you read. The story I tell everyone. It's like when I was talking to Ryan about the ancient poets. I determined what was worth telling or not. I determined who was a villain and who was a hero. Rewriting my own story made it bearable."

It's so dark in the room and my words float into nothingness.

"It's scary to realize what you really are. Not who you *say* you are, but who you *really* are."

What does that make me, I think?

A survivor.

Or a ghost.

Maybe Emily Duran did die in the jungle. Her body came back, but not her soul.

"You might wonder, why didn't I just tell the truth about killing Derek? People would understand—my shock, fear, Derek going crazy. But I think when I got back here, I felt bad for him. He hated his life. I wanted to give him a good ending, better than the one he really had. Like mine. Maybe in death, if only at the end, people will remember him for doing what was right.

Maybe that makes up for everything that led up to it. A final act of forgiveness. We all need forgiveness, don't we?"

"Or maybe," I laugh. "It was guilt. All the time I sat telling his mother he saved my life, I had to restrain myself from blurting out, 'I killed him! I killed your son! I bashed his head in with a rock until he didn't look human anymore.'"

There are so many lies. I am drowning in lies.

"When the boar was killing Ryan? I never picked up a piece of bamboo and waved it off. No, I stayed right there, listening to his screams. I can hear them now. I was terrified. And that boar, it didn't kill him right away. It took its time. It would gore him and then step back, like a cat toying with a mouse. Going back and forth, protecting its turf. All through it Ryan screamed for help. The boar finally got a piece of him, a *piece of meat* and walked off. That's when the screaming stopped."

I try to shake the image away.

"The only thing that makes me feel better? No one else did anything, either. We were all cowards that day."

It's so quiet I can hear the ticking of the analog clock.

"When Nico fell and I went down the cliff to see him? I didn't go to say good-bye. I went to get the bag of food. I was hungry. And you know what? I did eat it. I wasn't going to save it for *them*. I ate the last few mushrooms while I climbed up. It wasn't many. Maybe two or three stems. But Derek was right to accuse me."

"I don't know who ate the food in the night, though. That's the thing I don't know. It wasn't me. Maybe it was all of us, slowly sneaking a piece or two. And not that this makes up for anything, but it was me who thought of making a stretcher for Ryan. I carried him. No one else wanted to. Maybe in some small way that makes a difference."

I hope so, I think. I sure as hell hope so.

"As for sleeping with Nico, it's true it only happened once."

I pause, waiting for a sign, a response, something from my mother.

"I slept with the guy my best friend liked. What kind of girl does that? You hate those girls. *I* hate those girls. No one grows up thinking that's who you'll be. And then it happens. And you're like, oh, that girl is me. How did I become the villain in my own life? At the time, I didn't know why I'd done what I did. Now I do. I was jealous of Viv. I wanted to feel special. I wanted something she didn't have. And after I was with him, I knew, deep down, I'd been there first. I literally felt his heartbeat in my hand. I finally had something she didn't."

The hospital is so sterile. Unlike me.

"Not a satisfying answer, but it's the truth. And what started as my own little secret began to eat away at me. I swallowed that secret and kept it buried. No one was ever going to know. Especially Viv.

"What hurts more, though, were Nico's last words. They weren't 'the sun feels nice.' How nice would that have been? Makes dying seem, well, not like it was. His last words were pleading with me not to leave. Begging me. I left him waiting for death. I left him in fear. Remember how I spent that one summer volunteering at the Humane Society? I only lasted a few days. I couldn't bear to be around when they put the animals down. What was worse was when people would just drop off their old dogs knowing what would happen to them. They threw away their dogs like garbage. I hated those people. But I did that to Nico. I left him there. Alone."

I stop and take a long breath. I am so tired.

"That's the thing with secrets. They always come out. I guess that's why I'm telling you. I'll say it once so I know it's out in the universe. No one else may know, but I do. I know the secret's not a secret anymore. Maybe it won't kill me so much when I think about it."

My mother sits across from me, slumped over, but her breathing has changed. It's no longer deep, but shallow. Her eyes are closed, but I know she's only pretending to sleep. I don't know how long she's been listening. That's fine, I think. We all have our secrets. Now she has mine.

"I think that's everything," I say. "Well, almost everything."

The flight had been smooth, and yet I waited in tense anticipation for the turbulence to return. I reminded myself: *not much longer. We're almost there.*

As a distraction, I thought of the book of poetry Johannes had given me, a cherished gift, which rested in my bag like a permanent valentine. In my row, Viv sat in her chair, sleeping, and I was jealous that her life seemed non-stick; everything that slapped against it simply fell to the wayside.

I took deep breaths to try and calm myself.

The air in the cabin was dry and it was like breathing from inside a scuba-diving tank. I just wanted off this plane. I tapped Johannes on the shoulder.

"I gotta use the ladies' room."

That's when we heard a loud mechanical snap. The plane began to vibrate. It reminded me of the awful sound in cars when the windows are down and it's like someone blowing over an empty beer bottle.

"Is that normal?" I asked.

The look on his face told me it wasn't, but he lied to soothe me. "I'm sure it's nothing."

I decided to stay in my seat.

Things happened quickly. The plane jostled violently, and not like rhythmic turbulence, more like a bobber being pulled down by a creature you never want to see. We descended unnaturally, too fast, too steep. Fasten Seat Belt Lights snapped on. The captain yelled over the intercom: "Seatbelts! Seatbelts!"

This wasn't normal. This wasn't normal at all.

People were screaming, and I felt the G-forces pressing me against my seat. Strangely, I felt as if I was in the center of an emotional hurricane. Around me, chaos reigned, but in my own little world, I watched with surreal calmness. All sound faded to nothing. People's mouths were agape, their faces like caricatures, drawings an artist would make on the seashore, exaggerating features.

The plane not only vibrated: it rumbled, and I felt the low-grade pulses rising through the soles of my feet, to my legs, shaking my entire body. It was as if the plane's very skeleton was coming apart and it was fighting to remain whole. The bins atop the plane came loose and suitcases fell. Up and down the aisle bags rained down, some opening, throwing out clothes like confetti in a parade. The emergency lights popped on while other lights flickered. The

TV screens in the back of our seats went to static, flooding the cabin in a ghostly hue.

In my mind, I transposed the people screaming in terror into people at a club, dancing, their hands waving in the air, their mouths open as if singing.

Johannes shook me, and it brought me back to reality.

He was a grown man and I saw his pants were wet. He screamed at me, "You're my wish, Emily! You're my wish!" He reached over and tried to kiss me, but with all the turbulence, it was impossible, our heads colliding. Frustrated, he unbuckled his seat belt and grabbed the back of my head and kissed me long and hard on the lips.

"I love you, Emily. I love you."

Those were the last words he ever said to me.

We dropped so much I felt my hair rise above my head and Johannes flew from his seat, hitting the ceiling. Almost just as fast, the altitude shifted and he dropped back to his seat, his head bloody, and I thought with envy, unconscious.

Viv cried across from me.

I made the mistake of looking out the window. All was a vast emptiness. I didn't see a single town or road. We were falling into the middle of nowhere.

There was nowhere to go. Nowhere to run.

Nothing to do but wait.

I thought of my wish, the wish Johannes promised I could send into the heavens, and I mentally sent it as far and fast and hard as I could: *I don't want to die. Someone else, but not me.*

After we fell from the sky, after the plane had crashed, after I'd been pushed from the sinking aluminum tube and into the water, I was dead to the world and when I came to I was drowning. Water gushed into my mouth and I was tumbling, flailing, not knowing what end was up or down. I heard the sounds of screaming and the roaring of water and then nothingness. I was in a river.

The current sped faster, churning like boiling water and I thought I was going to die. The torrent sucked me into a watery hell and I couldn't breathe. I started to panic.

Suddenly, I took a shot to the head and saw stars. A high-pitched squeal rang in my ears. A growing sensation of darkness invited me to join its depths. I could let go. I could fall into it, like falling asleep. How badly I wanted to sleep.

I was about to when something grabbed me. My head was pulled out of the water. I looked and only saw the sun reflecting behind someone's head. The face came into focus. "Viv?"

"I've got you, Emily."

My head was woozy. This tiny person was swimming with me. She said, "Can you kick a little?"

I listened like a child and did as she asked. She was so beautiful in that light. Her hands around me. Helping me. Saving me. I said, "You look like an angel."

"Nothing close. Keep kicking, Emily. We're almost there."

Viv was no mirage. She helped me onto shore and I thought of her as an ant that could lift several times its body weight. She gently sat me down in the mud. Scrunched with concern, her face was right in front of mine, "You took a shot to the head."

"I never told you, Viv. I love you. You're my best friend."

"I love you, too, Emily. Now rest." She laid me on the ground. "Everything's gonna be all right."

And I knew it would be. My best friend was by my side.

CHAPTER THIRTY-THREE

The interviews are over and the world knows. Not the truth maybe, but the truth the world *wants* to hear. A story that makes people believe in hope. Alan put the kibosh on doing any more so as not to saturate the market. Just enough, he said, to tease the audience, get the story out there, and then move onto a book deal. He said we'd use my journal as raw material. We meet publishers next week, and the week after, movie studios. The future awaits.

I'm feeling better. Confessing was like shedding skin, like a molting snake. I was lost but now I'm found. I am forgiving myself and I feel lighter and lighter.

It's odd: the crash was bad luck, but I was rescued by good luck. The search, after all, had been canceled. We were declared dead. But a helicopter on the payroll of a wealthy Riverdale Academy parent found me. Pete Conlin's parents, in fact. It was purely by chance that the pilot decided to check a route from off the grid before heading back to base. I plan on living off that stroke of luck for the rest of my life.

If there is forgiveness in death, then I think, surely I'm allowed forgiveness in life. I've decided to get my GED and then go to college. I'm leaving writing behind. Words on a page are all manipulation, anyway. Instead, I may go into psychology and trauma care. I know what trauma is, and I know how to move past it. Maybe I can help others.

No one changes. Not really. That's what Derek had said.

I've come to believe events don't change you; they *reveal* you.

And I know I am stronger than I ever believed.

If I've learned anything over the past few months, it's that we are all miserably flawed and capable of acting like monsters. And yet there's something in me determined to do something with this knowledge—rise about it, somehow.

As for today, this is to be my last in the hospital. With the interviews over, there's no need for "optics," and I can go home. I've only eaten hospital food, and I'm craving an In-N-Out Burger animal-style something fierce. I'm craving a walk on the beach. I'm craving a lot of things.

I'm no longer anonymous. Someone created a Facebook page in my honor. There are even a couple marriage proposals. So weird.

I've had so many days subtracted from my life that it's going to feel strange to go back to *living*. I'm scared, too. I know how ruthless the world can be and I'm stepping back into it. But I remind myself when I'm feeling anxious: I am a survivor. I know what it takes. No one will drown me. Ever.

I pack my meager things, mainly get-well cards and dried flowers. I gather them in my hand and they seem like remnants from someone else's life. Someone else's history. I let them fall into the wastebasket.

There's a knock at the door. "Come in," I say.

The door opens a few inches. The bottom feet of a wheelchair tries to push through. Someone's arm swings the door wide open, and the girl in a wheelchair awkwardly pushes herself inside. She's too slow and the door clanks against metal. Attached to the chair is a clear bag, from which snakes a plastic drip-tube into her forearm.

The girl is small, her head shaved, her cheeks hollow, and she looks like an anorexic patient from an eating disorder clinic. She wears a blue hospital gown, but there are clean bandages wrapped around her arms and legs. One arm is in a fresh cast. She wears a patient barcode bracelet on her wrist that looks brand new. She must've been admitted today. I'm having an awful sense of déjà vu, but I know I haven't lived this moment before. She looks familiar, but I can't place her. I wonder if she's wandered into the wrong room, or maybe this is hers and the hospital thinks I've already left.

"I'll be out of your way in just a sec," I say.

"Don't you recognize me?" she asks, her voice like pebbles against a lake.

That voice. I stop and look at her. I really have no clue. No clue at all, unless....

It couldn't be.

My heart stops.

The silky dark hair is gone. The infectious smile is gone. In its place is someone—*something*—else.

Is it? Could she have survived? Could they have found her?

My legs slip out from under me and I sit on the bed, dazed. "Viv, is that you?"

She nods, and there's the slightest smile on her gaunt face, like a shrunken apple left too long in the sun. I have a flood of questions and concerns but before I can ask, she says, "I hear you have a story to tell."

The End

Thank you for making it all the way to the end of this book. If you'd like to know when I release a new one, sign up at my website jamesmorriswriter.com. I will only contact you when I have a new book! Also, if you enjoyed this, I'd love if you left a review and told a friend. Word of mouth is the best advertising around, and it helps allow me to do what I do. Serious gratitude and thanks!

ACKNOWLEDGEMENTS

I gratefully acknowledge the assistance of Bev Rosenbaum, Kristy Ellsworth, Emilia Rhodes, Julia Kenny, Carol Wentz, Helen Wentz, Jan Lauer and Jeannie Mountford for their valuable feedback. Much of the research was found on YouTube, including instructional videos from survivalists. Unfortunately, at the time, I did not write down the creators' names and thus, cannot give them proper attribution. But I thank the now-anonymous jungle adventurers for allowing me to populate my manuscript with moments of realism. As for the title, *Feel Me Fall*, I happily lifted it from the bandography in Frank Portman's novel *King Dork*. Once again, this book would not be possible without the support, encouragement and sharp editorial notes from my better half, Melissa.

ALSO BY JAMES MORRIS

What Lies Within

Melophobia

Abraham Lincoln Must Die

Made in the USA
Columbia, SC
06 June 2017